BE VIGILANT!

STRATEGIES TO STOP COMPLACENCY, IMPROVE PERFORMANCE, AND SAFEGUARD SUCCESS.

YOUR BUSINESS AND RELATIONSHIPS DEPEND ON IT

BY LEN HERSTEIN

contactus@managecamp.com

ISBN: 978-1-7370991-0-9 (print)
ISBN: 978-1-7370991-1-6 (ebook)

Ordering Information:
Special discounts are available on quantity purchases by corporations, associations, and others. For details, email contactus@managecamp.com.

Get the most from Be Vigilant!

Download a free Vigilance Check worksheet to use
as you read the book AND get your free Be Vigilant swag at:

BeVigilantBook.com/Vigilance-Swag/

TABLE OF CONTENTS

FOREWORD

By Melissa Agnes, founder and CEO, Crisis Ready Institute

2020 AND THE LACK OF CRISIS READINESS

When the COVID-19 pandemic hit in early 2020, my phone was ringing off the hook. Nearly every past conference organizer and event planner who had hired me over the past 10 years was calling to ask me to come back and speak with their audiences again. I remember a friend saying to me at the time, "You must be so thrilled to be getting all this work." But here's the thing, I wasn't thrilled. I was frustrated.

I was frustrated with the fact that I had already shared my time and spoken with these audiences. I had already given them insight and implementable actions to build into their business strategies so that, come a crisis, they would be—you guessed it—ready.

And they chose not to act.

They were inspired in the moment, they enjoyed the experience of my keynote, but it wasn't enough to help motivate them to take the simple yet profound actions I had recommended—actions and insights that would have helped them mitigate much of their vulnerability and thrive despite the pandemic.

On the other hand, the organizations that had been working with me for several years leading up to the pandemic *were* crisis ready come 2020. Moreover, through their trained vigilance, by the time the virus hit North America, they weren't just ready, they were *ahead*. They had evaluated the different ways in which COVID could impact their business—from short-term issues, straight through to impossible-to-imagine long-term catastrophic outcomes—and they had their diversified strategies of response in place.

I remember feeling profoundly proud of them. Their vigilance and refusal to avoid the inevitable meant they were in a position to rise as leaders for their stakeholders and communities amidst one of the scariest moments of our time.

While there are many ways in which we can count the differences between these two types of mindsets and organizations, one thing is evident: Those who put themselves in a position to thrive through the pandemic were vigilant. Those who found themselves in a reactionary mode, constantly trying to catch up and never feeling "in control" had been complacent, even despite the telltale signs as COVID traveled from Asia, through Europe and, inevitably, across the Atlantic.

COMPLACENCY IS HUMAN NATURE

We all want to feel comfortable and in control and, as success grows, it's easy to become overconfident and self-satisfied, ultimately leaving us increasingly exposed to new risks and vulnerabilities. Within this book, Len refers to this concept as "survivorship bias."

Survivorship bias is a reality that I see *all the time* in my line of work. Unfortunately, it's also a reality that we have all felt the repercussions of throughout the global pandemic, because, as Len also writes in this book, "Complacency kills."

Complacency kills businesses (Kodak and Blockbuster are among several examples Len provides), it kills relationships when couples stop being attentive and allow themselves to simply settle, and in its most drastic form, complacency kills people—as COVID has proven at far-too-big a scale.

Oftentimes, people are hesitant to be vigilant out of fear of living in paranoia. But, as Len puts it, the opposite of complacency is not paranoia, it's vigilance. Vigilance to keep our eyes on the horizon, to keep our fingers on the pulse, and to create the ability to be agile enough to thrive through change and challenge.

Contrary to complacency, vigilance saves businesses, it saves relationships, and it saves lives.

BUILDING YOUR VIGILANCE SKILLSET

Fortunately, the vigilance skill is one we can all learn and put to great use. In the pages ahead of you, Len draws from his experiences as a marketer, an entrepreneur, and a volunteer police officer, sharing stories that will keep you on the edge of your seat and help drive the points home. He then translates those very points and provides tactical ways to apply the lessons to your business and your personal life.

In my role as a Crisis Ready Expert who sits at many leadership tables around the world, I can say that there's never been a better time to learn and hone this skill. The world has entered an era of change and challenge and those who adopt vigilance into their lives and business strategies are going to be the ones who will prevail over the coming years.

Furthermore, one of the many lessons that has come forth due to the global pandemic is how drastically the world needs vigilant leaders who are equipped and confident to rise and lead through times of challenge and crisis—and there's no reason why that leader shouldn't or couldn't be you.

Len's perspective on complacency and vigilance provides a relatable way of helping you, the reader, strengthen your ability to protect the success you work so hard to attain. Because, as Len said when he introduced this book to me, "Achieving success is not the end goal. Keeping it is."

To your strengthened resilience and continued success,

Melissa Agnes, founder and CEO, Crisis Ready Institute

CHAPTER ONE

___

Complacency: A Threat Born From Success and Over-Confidence

In the police academy, we would dissect videos of calls that had started out routine but turned very bad. A traffic stop. A conversation with one half of a domestic dispute. A meal out. They had all turned very deadly, very quickly.

We discussed what went wrong. The lessons were clear and painfully obvious (with the benefit of hindsight and the safety of a classroom). We critiqued details we noticed, such as the officers' approach to the car, their body language, and how close they allowed the other party to get to them. We saw tiny clues from the suspect's body movements and eye glances.

And every student sat there and thought, "Not me. Never."

You may have thought the same if you've read case studies of Kmart, Blockbuster, Kodak, Borders, Sears, Circuit City or other once-successful brands that ultimately failed. In hindsight, the failures were so avoidable that you might get angry. How could they have been so blind? How could those companies have fallen so far, so fast?

Complacency kills.

HEY, LET'S NOT GET COMPLACENT OUT THERE!

If I had to choose just one word that's had the most significant effect on my recent life, it would be complacency. I'm conscious of it always. This awareness protects me from danger. It's helping to save my business. It strengthens my marriage and other relationships in my life. I truly believe that understanding it and how to manage it is the secret to success and happiness. It's a word that's very personal to me, and now I'm going to share it with you.

When I Google the word "complacent," I get over 24,700,000 results. The word is used *a lot*. You've probably used it recently. At the very least, you've heard it. We all think we know what it means. We can all use it in a sentence.

Normally, it's used as a warning. Maybe you're a football coach and your team's on a winning streak. You might say something before the game such as, "Hey! Let's not get complacent out there!" Or maybe your team at work just had a couple of big wins. As you cut the cake and congratulate everyone, you throw in a quick, "Let's not get complacent now," for good measure.

Now that I've brought up the subject, you'll hear someone else use the word today—in the news, in your office, at home. People throw the word around *all the time* because people understand it's something to avoid—but they rarely cover *how* to avoid it. We're all guilty of complacency. It's almost impossible not to be. It's all around us—

public health, marketing, life. It feeds on success, overconfidence, and faulty logic. And it's dangerous.

We've heard it nonstop during the coronavirus pandemic, especially when there has been perceived success. On March 12, 2021, over a year after the pandemic began, and in the wake of the UK seeing "34% of the adult population receiving at least one shot" of a vaccine, a story ran on Bloomberg entitled "The U.K.'s Next Covid Challenge Could Be Complacency."[1]

And it's not just pandemics. Complacency is discussed in great detail in all aspects of business and marketing failures. We can easily rattle off the names of once-huge companies that have fallen by the wayside—knocked off by competition they should have seen coming, or they saw coming and ignored out of hubris. We've seen how it can lead to human resources and public relations nightmares.

In November 2019, for example, Steve Easterbrook, who had been the CEO of McDonald's since March 2015, was fired when an inappropriate personal relationship with one of his employees came to light. In a subsequent lawsuit, the board of McDonald's alleged that "[h]e violated the Company's policies, disrespected its values, and abused the trust of his coworkers, the Board, our franchisees, and our shareholders."[2]

The CEO of McDonald's! Evidently, he was "morally bankrupt," but managed to lead McDonald's for over four and a half years without anybody noticing or doing anything about it? How does stuff like this happen? Do you ever think about that?

I certainly didn't. Not until I became a police officer—at the ripe age of 45. It was then I realized complacency is all around us. Always. And we don't notice it. We don't see it—until it's too late. And it's dangerous. Sometimes, deadly.

COMPLACENCY IS NOT JUST LAZINESS

To many, complacency means laziness. But that's not really accurate.

Merriam-Webster defines complacency as the following:

1. self-satisfaction especially when accompanied by unawareness of actual dangers or deficiencies. When it comes to safety, *complacency* can be dangerous.

2. an instance of usually unaware or uninformed self-satisfaction.[3]

So, complacency isn't so much laziness as it is smugness: self-satisfaction, an unawareness of actual dangers.

But how can a *cop* be unaware of dangers? How could Blockbuster not see the looming danger of the internet and streaming? How could doctors and governments not be prepared for a pandemic? How can two people who love each other not see that they are slowly drifting apart?

The answer is that overconfidence and success breed complacency. The irony is, the more success you've enjoyed, the more likely you are to become complacent.

In this book, we'll recognize how dangerous it is to us, our organizations, our brands, and our families. We'll understand where it comes from. And we'll learn techniques, battle tested in arguably the most dangerous breeding ground of complacency, that will help you combat it and keep it at bay.

OUT OF NOWHERE

At about 11:40 p.m. on January 7, 2016, Philadelphia Police Officer Jesse Hartnett was driving his marked patrol vehicle at 60th Street and Spruce Street in Philadelphia. That was when Edward Archer, a man who later pledged his allegiance to ISIS, rushed towards the vehicle and fired 13 shots at Officer Hartnett, at one point shoving his gun through the driver window. Hartnett was struck three times. Miraculously, he was able to both survive and return fire, hitting Archer while chasing him on foot. Archer, who was quickly apprehended (and later convicted of the attempted murder and sentenced to between 48-and-a half and 97 years in prison), had never met Officer Hartnett and had chosen him at random.[4]

Officer Hartnett's training, awareness, and quick and decisive action saved his life that night. By all accounts, things could have gone much worse. And it highlights why police officers can never really relax—always keeping their heads on a swivel and watching their backs.

Yet, even with that much at stake, police officers still get complacent every day. They get lulled into losing sight of the dangers around them. You'll read stories about it in this book. So, then, what hope does everyone else (businesspeople, lawyers, engineers, teachers, etc.) have of avoiding it?

Rest easy—it's not all gloom and doom. It's not even mostly gloom and doom. It turns out there are proven ways you can defend against complacency in all aspects of your life. And you can start doing it right now.

IT ALL STARTED WITH A FACEBOOK POST

As I mentioned, I didn't always think about complacency. For me, it all started with a Facebook post.

Douglas County Sheriff's Office
January 5, 2015

Ever dreamt about working in law enforcement? Our Reserve Deputy program lets you serve and protect in your free time.

The Douglas County Sheriff's Office is holding its first Reserve Deputy Academy to train residents who have the time, talent, and desire to wear a badge and help protect and serve… "We're looking for individuals who actively want to give back to their community," Sheriff Tony Spurlock says. "This isn't just about driving a patrol car. This is for people who really care about their community and can volunteer time to serve side-by-side with us." [5]

The fact was I had *not* dreamt of being a law enforcement officer. I had never really thought of it before. But I *was* looking for a way to give back to the community, and I did have a tremendous amount of respect for people who served the public. And, I'll be honest, this sounded pretty cool.

So, I ran it by my wife, got the okay, and then began a long and involved process. It first involved an orientation meeting attended by over 100 people, 95 percent of whom were younger than me, many with previous law enforcement or military experience. Then I had to complete a huge application that involved tracking down my high school transcript (from 1987!) and my college transcript, listing every place I had ever lived, noting anything I had ever done wrong, and providing several character references. It dawned on me that this process was probably easier for a 21-year-old than a 45-year-old!

Then came the agility test (also easier for a 21-year-old), the written test, an integrity interview, a very thorough background check, a medical test, and a psychological test. After all of that, I was one of about 25 people who were accepted into an academy that ran 26 weeks and about 310 hours, and culminated with my graduation and commission as a Reserve Peace Officer in the state of Colorado. This led to 440 hours of field training before I became certified and able to work on patrol solo—for free. Yep, that's right—I go out and work patrol (with the same authority as any full-time peace officer in Colorado) on my own for hundreds of hours a year for free.

Maybe right about now you're questioning my sanity. You're wondering why I would choose to do this *now*, especially for free? So, let's just get that out of the way.

I do it because I want to give back to my community and be part of solutions, not just be someone who complains about problems. I still believe, even with everything that has happened in this country in recent history, that there is no better way for me to do that than to serve honorably and genuinely try to help as many people as I can.

I'd be lying, though, if I said that, at several times throughout this process, my wife didn't start to question the validity of the psychological testing.

Over the years, I've have had really fun days, like when I responded to an actual call about a chicken crossing a road, was able to find said chicken, and even reunited the chicken with its rightful owner. As much as I wanted to, though, I couldn't find the chicken at first, which led to me having the opportunity to say the following on the radio to dispatch and the rest of the people on shift at the time:

"202-Adam. UTL on the chicken."

202-Adam was my designator for the day, and UTL means "unable to locate." It was, by far, the most fun thing I have ever gotten to say on the radio. It's not often you get to say something funny on the radio without getting reprimanded for wasting radio time. Fortunately, just after I finished calling out the UTL, that crazy chicken just meandered its way right in front of my patrol car! Don't worry; I didn't hit it, and the chicken was safely returned to its owner moments later.

I've also had some really bad days, like when I woke up on New Year's Eve 2017 to learn there had been a shoot-out between deputies and a man at an apartment complex on the north side of our county.

I rushed to get into uniform and get to the scene to help in any way I could. When I arrived, I quickly learned that Deputy Zackari Parrish had been shot and killed, and several other deputies had been wounded while trying to help a mentally troubled young man who had multiple high-powered weapons and hundreds, if not thousands, of rounds of ammunition.

Another really bad day was November 25, 2016, when I was working a single car accident on northbound Interstate 25. Two Colorado State Troopers showed up to take over the scene. I got back in my car and continued my patrol shift heading south. Before I reached the next exit, I was dispatched back to the scene for an Officer Down call. The minutes it took me to weave my way back through traffic with my lights flashing and sirens blaring were among the longest minutes of my life.

When I arrived, I found out that Colorado State Police Trooper Cody Donahue had been struck and killed by a semitruck just minutes after I left. I worked that scene for hours into the night, standing at attention and saluting as the SUV carrying Trooper Donahue's body drove by. And, when I finally got back to the office, I sat and cried for a long while. It wouldn't be the last time.

Between days like those, though, I've had many very fulfilling and satisfying ones helping the citizens of Douglas County during their times of need. Sometimes it's a medical call—administering Narcan to an unresponsive opioid overdose victim and seeing them miraculously wake up as if nothing ever happened. Sometimes it's a domestic violence call that results in a spouse and some children getting a much-deserved restful night of peace and safety while their abuser goes to jail. Sometimes it's just the pure joy of hanging out with some kindergarteners on the playground (and refusing, once more, their requests to get Tased). These all go in the "good day" column.

There are lots of crazy calls and stories to be told. The truth is, though, most calls are pretty routine, such as traffic stops, accidents, and thefts—exactly the types of calls that can dull the senses, generate overconfidence, and breed complacency, which can easily become deadly.

My previous nearly 30 years of work experience have been mostly in brand marketing. Since 2003, I've been running the company that produces the annual Brand ManageCamp marketing conference. Before that, I was in brand marketing with Campbell Soup, Coca-Cola, and Nabisco. Prior to that, I was a consultant with Andersen Consulting (now Accenture). The life I was used to involved strategy meetings, marketing plans, creative development, pricing, manufacturing, distribution, and a fair amount of business travel.

While on the surface, this seems worlds apart from my new gig in law enforcement, I discovered there was quite a bit of overlap. I started seeing things that I was learning and doing in law enforcement that could directly apply to my business and personal life. And I was fascinated by the lessons I learned.

The first, and perhaps most powerful, lesson was introduced on our first day of academy and then driven home every day since then:

Complacency kills.

Those words are on a sign we see every time we exit the Sheriff's Office parking lot. It sits right on a fence that must open before we can exit, staring us in the face every day.

The sign itself is from an initiative called Below 100 (www.Below100.com), and it's a reminder of our goal to get the number of law enforcement deaths per year down to below 100. If we could accomplish it, it would, unfortunately, be the first time in a very long time—since 1943, to be exact.

According to the Below 100 website, it appears that 100 is an arbitrary number meant to create a big stretch goal. The site says it was based on a statement made by Major Travis Yates of the Tulsa Police Department in April 2010 at a dinner during a law enforcement conference. The dinner conversation revolved around a recent increase in law enforcement deaths and Major Yates said, "If we would just slow down, wear our seatbelts, and clear intersections, we could get our line of duty deaths down to below 100 a year." And the concept of Below 100 was born.

The Below 100 sign focuses on some seemingly mundane concepts: Wear your belt, wear your vest, watch your speed, and WIN (What's Important Now?). But it closes with a powerful line:

REMEMBER: Complacency Kills!

In the academy, we were taught how police work can make you comfortable. It can lead to a false sense of security; a lulling of the senses; an unawareness of, or an unwillingness to address, lurking dangers—which could all very quickly lead to potentially deadly consequences.

To a bright-eyed and bushy-tailed cadet, not becoming complacent seemed as obvious as tying your shoes. As clear as things were in the academy, however, we soon discovered that the complacency starts to creep in the moment boots hit the streets, just as it does in corporate offices and households everywhere.

In law enforcement, we recognize the danger of complacency, and we work on identifying it and fighting it every day. I've experienced it over and over. I see it in the way a crime scene was approached, where a car was parked to type reports, and in a stance or a tone of voice. Battling complacency is a daily struggle for law enforcement, and there are many tools that we use to fight that battle.

Accept now that your risk for complacency is very real—and much higher than you ever thought. And, while the dangers in law enforcement are literally the difference between life and death, complacency can just as easily kill brands, businesses, and relationships. As I'll describe in the final chapter of this book, it nearly killed my own business.

Throughout this book, you'll become complacency conscious. I'll explain why complacency is so dangerous to you. I'll then cover very specific things you can do to identify complacency and combat it. These are tactics we use every day in law enforcement. Once you learn them, you'll find yourself immediately implementing them. None of these is rocket science; you just probably aren't utilizing them right now.

You'll notice that I spend the vast majority of this book focused on the implications for business. There are, of course, many opportunities to apply these same concepts to our personal lives and relationships. You'll likely make those personal connections yourself as you read each chapter. I plan to explore those more directly in future work.

Early in this chapter, I said that overconfidence and success breed complacency and that the more success you've enjoyed, the more likely you are to become complacent. There's a term for this: *survivorship bias.*

CHAPTER ONE VIGILANCE CHECK

Ask yourself:

1. What does it mean to be complacent? Why is it so dangerous?

2. What conditions or attitudes make complacency more likely?

3. What's the most recent example of complacency you've seen or experienced? What was the result?

4. Where are *you* most vulnerable to complacency? Where is your *business* most vulnerable? Where is your *family* most vulnerable?

CHAPTER TWO

Survivorship Bias: How Past Success Can Hurt You

I once was sent on a call of a very drunk man who had left a bar, ignoring pleas from others to not get in his truck, and driven away. Fortunately, they had written down his license plate. By the time I arrived, he had left the scene, so I went by the address associated with the plate.

As I drove up, I saw the truck in the driveway, nose right up to and leaning on the garage door. I rang the doorbell, and a man opened the door. He could barely stand; his breath smelled heavily of alcohol. His hair was all disheveled, and he had blood streaming down his forehead.

It didn't take much prompting for him to tell me the whole story. In very quick succession, he told me he had been drinking at the bar and had driven himself home. He had drunk a few beers while he was at the bar. He came straight home and didn't hit anything, he said. He hadn't had anything to eat, drink, or smoke since leaving the bar.

He wasn't aware of the blood until I asked him how he hurt himself and if he needed medical attention. At that point, he took his hand and rubbed it over his forehead and back through his hair, leaving a red trail. He said he fell out of the truck when he got home, and he had hit his head in doing so. I put on my gloves.

The man stepped out of the doorway, and my partner and I had to brace him to keep him from falling. Although he was leaning back against the door, it seemed unlikely he'd be able to stay on his feet.

Even with all of this, the man couldn't see what the issue was. He got very angry. "What's the problem? Why are you here?" he yelled at me. "I made it home, didn't I?"

In his mind, the outcome was positive, so he must not have done anything wrong. He'd probably done it plenty of times before. Each time, he'd been successful in his own mind: He'd arrived home safely and hadn't been caught. He hadn't caused any accidents (that he knew of).

Did you know that, on average, a drunk driver will drive under the influence 80 times before their first arrest?[6] But he didn't comprehend the danger he'd put himself and others in and was, unbelievable as it sounds, unaware of the potential dangers and of his own vulnerabilities. This is not uncommon for drunk drivers. In this case, survivorship bias can prove fatal.

I placed him under arrest. But, before I could take him to jail, I had to take him to the hospital for a scan of his head injury. In all, I think I spent about five to six hours with him. About four to five hours of that he spent yelling at me and insulting me. Here was my favorite:

"How old are you?" he asked in a boozy, slurred speech. "I'm 48,"

I replied. "Wow!" he came back, his bloodshot eyes widening. "I thought you were *much* older than that. You must've had a hard life." Ouch.

I smiled and refrained from any comeback. I did my time that night. And I won't lie—it's one of a few times that I've found myself thinking, "I do this for free?"

SURVIVORSHIP BIAS IS A LOGIC ERROR

Have you ever heard a person from one generation complaining about the fragility of the people from the next generation?

For my generation, it might go something like this:

"Concussion protocol? When I was playing ball growing up, you were either unconscious or you got back in the game. Now, every time two kids run into each other, we need to get a medical team and an MRI onto the field to do a full workup! I must've had five concussions as a kid. I was dizzy and the next day I was fine!"

The implication is that since I'm okay (or think I'm okay), what I did was okay. Of course, we can see the obvious flaws in this line of thinking. The source of the faulty thinking, survivorship bias, is a real thing that clouds the judgement of most of us at some point and is one of the most blatant causes of complacency.

Maybe you've experienced this in the workplace. You start a new job, and you come in fresh and full of vim and vigor. You've got ideas. You see loads of opportunity. You're going to change the world (or at least your little corner of it).

Then someone with more experience sits you down one day. The message you receive is that you should probably slow down a little. Take it easy. Look around—see all the people who've been here the longest or the ones who've been most successful? They're the ones who keep their heads down and do their work. Sure, there are a few who have popped their heads up and taken a chance and succeeded. But not many. It's too risky. The message you hear is, "Do your job and you can have a nice long career here like me."

You might start looking around and seeing that the people who are successful are not the ones who rock the boat. You might conclude that the advice is sage. What you're missing, though, are all the smart and ambitious people who left on their own because the environment was stifling. They left because they found it impossible to buck the system. And who knows how much better the company could have been if they had stayed and been nurtured? But all you see are those who accepted their fates and stayed. They won the battle of attrition, but they lost the war.

Survivorship bias is a logic error. It involves focusing attention and analysis only on people or things that have made it past some sort of qualifying or selection event—and ignoring those who didn't. By focusing only on successes and ignoring anything or anyone that failed (or left), you can see how the analysis can become optimistic. It can lead people to mistaking correlation for causality.

Essentially, survivorship bias means that the more you succeed, the more you believe that what you did worked. Think about that for a minute. The more successful you are, the more confident you become. You become less aware of potential threats or vulnerabilities and more in danger of becoming complacent.

In the above example, if success is seen as longevity in a position in the company, and by keeping your head down and not standing out you can achieve longevity, you might perceive success. And that success would lead you to become overconfident in your capabilities. Then that overconfidence could easily make you unaware of potential threats or vulnerabilities, both internal and external, to your team, your division, or your company. And, just like that, you've become complacent.

SURVIVAL DOESN'T MEAN SUCCESS

I saw a meme the other day. It said:

> *I SURVIVED: Spankings…Lead Paint…Rusty*
> *Playgrounds…Second-Hand Smoke…*
> *Toy Guns…No Seatbelts…No Helmets…Drinking*
> *from the Hose… 'SHARE' if you did too!*

You probably get the idea. If you didn't survive, you can't share! And, if you did survive, you might think all those things are okay. Lead paint? Second-hand smoke? No seatbelts? No helmets? Just because it worked out for you, that doesn't mean it was the right thing or the safe thing. Past success breeds overconfidence. And overconfidence is where the complacency virus grows best.

This is a problem for law enforcement officers. Most of the time, regardless of the attention paid to officer safety, things turn out fine. You've probably heard police work described as 99 percent boredom and 1 percent sheer terror. I don't like the word *boredom* in this fashion; I think it's more accurate to say the work is 99 percent unsurprising or routine. That means most calls end like you'd expect them to.

Say you get a call about a theft. It typically ends with a statement from the victim and a report—not boring, but not surprising either. You might go to 1,000 or 10,000 of those calls over the course of a career. You show up at the house, ring the doorbell, somebody opens the door and invites you in, you get the information you need, and then you leave. Easy peasy.

The success you have with those calls can breed the very same complacency that can become deadly in an instant. You're not taught in the academy or in field training to casually walk up to a door, ring the doorbell, and then stand in front of it. You're taught to tactically approach the door, keeping an eye and ear out for potential danger signs. Once you ring the bell or knock on the door, you then back out of the "funnel of death" that a doorway creates, ideally finding some level of physical cover to stand behind, because you never know if there's an ambush waiting for you on the other side of that door. What if it was all a ruse and there's a cop-hater waiting to open fire through the door?

After a thousand non-ambush calls, you can begin to see where it might be tempting for that officer to start backing away less and less from that door. Perhaps they start with not seeking cover, standing out in the open. Then they only take three steps back instead of 10. Eventually, they may ring that bell and stand right in front of that door. It's not that they're unaware of the potential dangers; it's just that their previous success has created a bias. They've convinced themselves that they can tell a dangerous call from a routine one— maybe based on the call notes they receive from the dispatcher, maybe based on the neighborhood, maybe based on the house or the cars in the driveway. But all those signals are just biases that create the false sense of lack of danger.

The problem is all this works…until it doesn't. Everything goes right until it goes wrong. And when it goes wrong, it goes very wrong.

At work, it could go something like this:

You look at the same metrics as they relate to sales in a team meeting every Monday. You look at yours and your competitors'. You look store-by-store, outlet-by-outlet. You look at price. You look at region. You look at promotion. And week after week, some of those metrics never change. Sales are steady, pricing is steady. Your competitors never do anything out of the ordinary. Your emails always have the same amount of opens and clicks. You get the idea.

So, you get comfortable. Maybe, the weekly meeting starts to seem unnecessary. Maybe, it starts to feel like you're just going through the motions.

So, you push the weekly meeting to every other week. Maybe even once a month. Look at all the time you've freed up!

Then something changes, and you no longer have the regular meeting to catch the anomaly. And, by the time you figure out what's changed, your business has suffered real damage.

We don't have to look far to find examples of survivorship bias in our personal lives, like when my daughter decides not to study for a test and gets an A. And then she does it again. By the third time, she's concluded that her *not* studying is a time-proven studying technique! When the bad grade inevitably comes, the ensuing shock on her part is genuine but misguided.

My least favorite examples of survivorship bias in one's personal endeavors revolve around child safety issues. Nothing makes my stomach turn more than seeing a car towing kids on sleds down the street after a fresh snow. The parent in that car is sure to brush you off if you were to try to intervene. "My parents did this for me and I've been doing it with my kids for years and nobody's ever been hurt," they might reply.

Then you read about the 11-year-old girl who died on November 27, 2020, "…after the sled she was riding on slammed into the back of a pickup truck that was towing her."[7] And it makes you sick.

So, what's the alternative? Paranoia? Forever walking around expecting the worst around every corner? No. The opposite of complacency isn't paranoia. It's vigilance.

DON'T BE PARANOID. BE VIGILANT. ALWAYS.

The main difference between paranoia and vigilance is this:

Paranoia is based in fear. Vigilance is based in awareness.

We don't need to be afraid of the potential of danger; we need to be aware of the possibility of danger. Without that awareness, one can become lulled into a false sense of security. That false sense of security results in a letting down of defenses as well as the development of blind spots. And that results in vulnerability.

Vulnerability combined with overconfidence and self-satisfaction can be a dangerous situation, whether it is in law enforcement, in business, or in life. It can make you temporarily blind to the very dangers you used to know existed. It can also make you a target for those aware of and looking for the signs.

Whether you know it or not, your complacency can be seen by those around you. It can be sensed by how you act and talk and conduct yourself. Vigilant competitors are looking for those signals and are ready to pounce when they see them.

We were often told in the academy the importance of keeping our uniforms pressed and shoes shined. It wasn't for inspections. It was because criminals can pick up on those clues as they size up their situation. They're more likely to challenge, flee from, or fight an officer who appears not to care about appearance than one who gives the impression of being buttoned up. In their minds, an officer who looks like a slacker probably is one—slow, uncaring, and unaware. The hint of complacency attracts challenge.

In 1992, the FBI published a report titled, "Killed in the Line of Duty: A Study of Selected Felonious Killings of Law Enforcement Officers."[8] It detailed the conclusions from a study that included 51 incidents of people who killed police officers. These incidents were committed by 50 distinct people and resulted in the deaths of 54 officers. It included an exhaustive review of all the circumstances of each killing, as well as interviews with the offenders.

One of the key areas of findings revolved around professional demeanor, and concluded that "officers should be aware of the body language and of other signals they are transmitting to the public." It details a case where an offender met two different officers in the same day. He evaluated each and chose to assault (and, sadly, kill) one but not the other.

In a second case, the offender "stated that he had evaluated the officer's behavior prior to taking aggressive action. He said, 'The officer was not authoritarian and did not take control of me. He was a willing participant in his death.'" The study suggested that an officer can change the outcome of their encounter with a criminal through the image they project.

It's the same in business. Is a startup more likely to challenge a company or industry that is vigilant and appears ready to actively defend itself? Or is it more likely to challenge a company or industry that looks to be asleep at the wheel?

Examples of this abound in business, especially when it comes to the idea of innovating around the boundaries of existing industries. Think about how Uber and Lyft and the idea of ridesharing has up-ended the industry of getting people from point A to point B.

For as long as I can remember, there were two options if people needed a ride somewhere and weren't going to take public transportation—taxi or car service (limo). Taking a taxi was seen as quick and easy (and relatively cheap), but perhaps low on quality and inconvenient in terms of payment methods. Riding in a limo was seen as more customized, more luxurious, and more prestigious, albeit more expensive and taking longer to procure. The lines were clear, and people and situations were clear-cut as to which was the more appropriate solution for the moment.

Over time, the technology that could make taxis more convenient and accessible became available, but the industry had become comfortable and overconfident. Their past success proved to them that what they were doing was right. Why innovate when people are willing to stand out in the rain and flag you down? Why take credit cards and pay fees when people can be forced to pay by cash? Why dispatch via computer when you can communicate over a squelchy CB radio?

In New York City, the most difficult aspect of getting into the taxi business was getting a medallion, which is essentially a transferable permit that allows a taxi to operate. At their peak, they could be priced at over $1 million![9] And why not? Once someone got a medallion, they were pretty much guaranteed business. The rules of engagement were set, and if they followed the laws, they didn't have to worry too much about customer satisfaction. This was survivorship bias at its finest.

Ridesharing changed all that. Now you can order a ride that shows up within minutes. The fare is preset based on supply and demand. The payment is handled automatically. You can choose the level of comfort you would like. Drivers compete for business; they might even provide waters or mints. Some show movies or allow you to choose your music. They have chargers for every type of phone. The lines between taxi and car service have become blurred, and the need for either of them is now in question.

Sure, there are now apps where you can order taxis, pay for them, take care of your tipping, etc. But all that came after Uber when the damage could no longer be contained.

This didn't happen by accident. Uber started in 2009 as an app to order black car limo-type rides. Not long after its launch in San Francisco, Uber could see it was connecting with tech-savvy urban professionals. In 2011, Uber rolled out in New York City. In both places it was met with heavy resistance from the established taxicab industry.[10]

The amount of pushback was telling. The taxi industry had become vulnerable, and yet, it appears there was little vigilance in trying to understand where that vulnerability might be. Thinking back to those days in New York City, you could almost smell the vulnerability every time you got in a taxi.

And so, survivorship bias is a nasty, nasty enemy. First off, it's bred from success. Just the sheer fact of being successful puts you at an infinitely higher level of risk of becoming complacent. You just don't hear of too many flailing startups suffering from complacency!

Secondly, when complacency does appear, it's a super sharp double-edged sword. Not only can it fight you from within—making you more likely to slip up and make dangerous mistakes—but it also sends signals to your competition, to those who wish you harm. It's like a beacon flashing, inviting them to attack.

So, now that we've established that you're probably at higher risk of complacency than you thought, and that complacency is bad, the rest of this book is about how we can put ourselves in the best position to recognize and fight complacency. It's about how to remain vigilant and how to project that vigilance. And it's based on principles and practices I've learned through my experience in law enforcement.

It's my hope that you'll find these all immediately understandable and relatable, and you'll quickly start to see how you can apply them in both your professional and personal lives. Each chapter will include stories from law enforcement that you'll immediately find applicable to your own scenarios.

I encourage you to use these chapters as a resource you can keep coming back to, because the battle against complacency is a never-ending one. And once you get a little overconfident that you've got complacency beat—well, that's when you are, once again, most vulnerable!

So, let's start talking about how vigilance can save us from the complacency that is always nipping at our heels.

CHAPTER TWO VIGILANCE CHECK

Ask yourself:

1. Where are you most overconfident?

2. What examples can you find of your own survivorship bias at work and/or at home?

3. What are the potential risks of that survivorship bias?

4. What is the opposite of complacency?

CHAPTER THREE

Threat Awareness: You Can't Protect Against the Danger You Never See

On April 19, 2018, Deputy Taylor Lindsey, 25, and Sergeant Noel Ramirez, 29, of the Gilchrist County Sheriff's Office in Florida were having a meal together—on duty and in uniform—at the Ace China Restaurant in Trenton, Florida. Deputy Lindsey had been on the job for two years. Sergeant Ramirez, a husband and a father of two, was a seven-year veteran.

At about 3 p.m., 59-year-old John Hubert Highnote walked into the restaurant carrying a rifle and killed both officers before they had a chance to return fire. Highnote then walked out of the restaurant to his car where he died by suicide.

While anti-police propaganda was later found in Highnote's home, the Gilchrist County Sheriff stated, "No clear motive has been established." Highnote was not on local law enforcement's radar, and there was no indication he personally knew either of his victims. He just knew they were wearing law enforcement uniforms.[11]

Obviously, these officers had no warning of what was coming. There's no way they could have known Highnote's intentions or even that he was there in the first place. In law enforcement, when we hear of a situation like this, we grieve the loss and then we study it, looking for anything we can glean that might help us avoid a similar circumstance. They obviously didn't see the potential danger coming their way, so how can we learn from their tragedy?

In August 2019, two off-duty Montreal police officers (who happened to be brothers) were attacked while out for a meal. They were walking along the street when a group of six people sitting at a nearby patio recognized them as officers.

"They were walking to go have a bite and someone recognized them on a terrace, yelled out, 'civilian police, civilian police,' and the next thing they knew they were being circled and punched and thrown to the ground," Inspector Marie-Claude Dandenault told reporters.

It seems that both officers policed the area they were in, and the people who attacked them were familiar to the authorities. But no specific motive was mentioned, other than their being police officers.[12]

Incidents like these are not uncommon and now dictate the way I (and most officers) approach eating out in public.

EATING OUT WITH ME IS NO PICNIC

When I walk into a restaurant, I immediately survey the dining room. Where are the exits? Where are the windows? Where's the entry to the bathrooms? Where's the entry to the kitchen? Is there anybody here I recognize?

Within a few seconds, I've already determined the tables where I'm willing to sit. I won't (if I can help it) sit where I am in any of the following situations:

- Have my back to anyone, including the waitstaff and kitchen personnel.

- Can't see the exits.

- Am in front of or near a window to the outside.

- Can't exit from the seat and engage a threat quickly.

As you can imagine, this limits things quite a bit. It annoys my children, because it usually means if we're at a table that is half booth and half chairs, I must sit on the booth part. And I must be on the outside seat—the one that allows me the ability to get up and move if needed.

It annoys my wife, because it means we can't sit at a free table in the middle of the restaurant where every chair has some blind spots. Obviously, I make some exceptions, but if possible, I avoid it.

Recently, my family and I went to a local breakfast spot. After waiting 20 minutes to get called for a table and then being led through the restaurant, I realized that the hostess was about to sit us at a table right in the middle of the entire place! Meanwhile, as I scanned the room, I recognized that a booth in the far corner was almost available. I asked the hostess if we could have that table instead. She agreed but said it would take a few minutes to clean it up, so she walked us back to the waiting area. My wife and kids were *not* happy.

This might sound like paranoia to you, but it isn't. It's a recognition that eating in public is a very vulnerable situation for a law enforcement officer—most certainly if you're in uniform, but even if you're off duty and not in uniform. Especially if you live in the area you patrol, you're likely to come across people you've pulled over, arrested, or just interacted with on a bad day. And it's far more likely that they'll recognize you than you'll recognize them. They may be patrons, or they may be employees. They may even just be strangers walking past the restaurant, looking to settle a beef you know nothing about. But the only way you may get an idea that they know you or somehow have a problem with you is when you see how they look at you.

Let's face it—being out, having a meal with your family or friends, is not the time you would expect yourself to be particularly aware of everything going on around you. There are distractions. Your companions expect (rightfully so) your attention and your participation. You might be enjoying an adult beverage (or three). It's very easy to become complacent and fall into a state of unawareness of potential danger.

That's why it's so important that I situate myself in a way that makes the detection of danger as easy as possible. By identifying all the potential places that danger could approach from and positioning myself in a way where I can passively have eyes on those places so nobody can sneak up on me, I significantly increase the likelihood that I can identify danger. The faster I'm able to spot a potential issue, the more likely I can deal with it safely.

From the previous examples, you might be thinking, "What could the officers have done differently? How were they complacent here?" The point is, we're not looking to place blame or find where they went wrong. Complacency is very rarely something that you can pinpoint to a specific act or a specific point in time. However, when we analyze the situation, law enforcement officers will look for where they might have let their guard down and how and why that happened. Had they naturally fallen into a false sense of security? What would we do differently?

I'll be honest with you. It's very rare that I choose to eat in a public restaurant while in uniform. If I do, I'm hyper-aware of where I'm sitting, who's there, who's by the windows or doors, etc. Would I be this way if I hadn't learned from tragedies or incidents like those described above? Probably not.

Fighting complacency is a constant battle that requires unwaning vigilance. Complacency is a sneaky and conniving foe that's difficult to defeat. So, we don't look to place blame on officers when it happens. We understand why it does. We just try to use that knowledge to help us continue our own fight.

THE WORST TIME TO FIGURE OUT WHAT YOU'RE GOING TO DO IN A TIME OF CRISIS IS WHEN THE CRISIS HAS ALREADY BEGUN!

The stories I've told are, unfortunately, just a few of many. They're chilling and sobering, for sure. They're shown to us in the academy and in training throughout our careers, not to scare us or depress us, but instead to illustrate the risks involved if we let our guards down. We use them to discuss ways in which we can avoid or mitigate these types of risks, and they're meant to live within us so that we never forget.

When we discuss these incidents, we talk about more than the need to identify where the potential threats could come from. We also address the need to pre-think how we might handle those threats if they do appear. We do this because the worst time to figure out what you're going to do in a time of crisis is when the crisis has already begun.

What will I do if I recognize someone on the waitstaff as a person I've arrested? What if someone recognizes me and comes up to my table while my children are there? What if an altercation starts in the restaurant? What will it take for me to get involved as opposed to being a good witness? What should my wife and children do if something transpires?

Asking these questions is vigilance, not paranoia. Off-duty officers always have these thoughts in the back of their mind—and for good reason.

In September 2020, just before midnight, attackers fired seven shots into the home of a family in Camden, New Jersey. The husband and wife were both police officers, and an infant was also in the house. Authorities believed it was a targeted attack.[13]

Also in September 2020, "Ulster County (NY) District Attorney David J. Clegg held a press conference to address recent incidents of harassment and targeting of off-duty police officers and their families. 'There have been four incidents of off-duty police and their families being targeted, surveilled, and on one occasion, victimized by criminal mischief,' Clegg said."[14]

If it can happen at home, it can certainly happen at more public places like restaurants, where you're more likely to encounter a lot of people at once.

I've worked potential scenarios in my head countless times so that I won't have to think about it if or when it happens. Neither will my wife or children, because I've also addressed with them what they are to do—when they should run, when they should hide behind me, when they should call 911, and what they should say.

For example, if I had to engage in something that involved drawing my weapon, they know to let the dispatcher on the phone know who I am and what I'm wearing so I don't get mistaken for a suspect and get myself shot by accident.

POLICE CARS SIDE-BY-SIDE—GOOFING OFF OR BEING VIGILANT?

One of the most vulnerable times when we're on duty is when we're doing paperwork. They don't show it on TV or in the movies, but *a lot* of law enforcement work—especially on patrol—is paperwork.

By the nature of the job, we write most of our reports while in our cars when we have some downtime between calls. It's difficult to write a report *and* remain vigilant about what's going on around you. So, we try to park our cars in low-traffic areas, backing into areas where there are walls around us if possible.

Sometimes, you'll see two police cars parked side by side facing different directions. You may think those cops are just wasting time, shooting the breeze. Likely, though, they are watching each other's sixes (backs) while one or both take care of some paperwork. We understand where the threats could come from, and we set ourselves up to be able to see them and react if necessary. By lining up the cars that way, each officer just needs to be responsible for what's in front of them and to their right, as opposed to having to monitor 360 degrees.

We already know what we're going to do if a threat appears. If someone starts walking towards our cars, how are we going to address them and ensure the situation is as safe as possible for us? If a car approaches, how are we going to maneuver so we're not blocked in and we can maintain tactical positioning? The time to figure that out is not as someone is approaching. It's *well* before, when heads are clear and stress levels are low.

The other day, I was towards the close of a swing shift (which ends at midnight), and I had some paperwork to finish up. I went to the back end of a large parking lot at one of our local recreation centers. I backed into the spot so that I had a view of the entire parking lot and all the possible entry points. There was no reason for any other cars to be there at that time, and I was certain to see any that came in.

One did come in. When doing my paperwork, I consciously force myself to look up and around every few moments, so I immediately noticed a car driving through the lot and then turning to make its way towards me. My car was already in drive as I watched the vehicle start its approach. I got on the radio and let dispatch know I was going to be in contact with a suspicious vehicle, triggering another car to start my way with some urgency. I described the vehicle and the fact that it appeared to have just one occupant.

When it became clear that the vehicle was coming to me, I turned on all my overhead lights, as well as my spotlights—making it difficult for the other driver to see. The vehicle pulled off into a parking spot and shut down. I could see the driver clearly and left my vehicle to make contact, with my hand positioned to draw my weapon if I needed it.

It turns out that the driver was a teenage female who was just looking to report a friend of hers missing. There was no danger to me this time. However, there was also no way to know that until I knew. I had played out a scenario like this many times in my head. All my actions and options were pre-planned when stress levels were low, so I was able to stay focused on the potential threat without having to devise options and strategies on the fly.

THREAT IDENTIFICATION AND SCENARIO PLANNING FOR YOUR WORLD

Now let's apply these strategies to you. You may have already started the process, but let's bring it home.

First, you need to identify where any threats may come from. Identify the obvious ones, but also find your blind spots so you can eliminate them.

Risks could come from current competitors or future competitors, including companies, categories, and innovations that don't exist yet or haven't been on your radar. For example, Tesla's move from being an automaker to a sustainable energy company had broad implications for lots of folks, such as solar panel companies.[15]

Think Blockbuster and Netflix. Kodak and digital cameras. Toys "R" Us and Amazon (or Borders and Amazon or really *any* bricks-and-mortar store and Amazon), Nokia and iPhones, Uber and taxis, or any of the other familiar stories of the incumbent who got beat by the company, product, service, technology, or person they never saw coming. Or, maybe they saw it coming and just didn't recognize it as a threat.

Risks can emerge from other geographical regions. What effects will your business see from foreign competition? How might that change over time? Think cars (American versus Japanese, starting in the 1990s), computers (Dell and HP versus Asian competition in the form of Lenovo and the introduction of the Netbook by Asus and Acer), planes (US-based Boeing versus European Airbus), etc.

Risks can come from current or future legislation. Economic factors. Consumer demographic shifts. Psychographic shifts. Once-in-a-hundred-years worldwide pandemics. The threats can come from a lot of places.

Have you identified them all? Do you have eyes on them? Who in your organization is responsible for identifying those threats, for making everyone else aware of them, for eliminating blind spots, and for developing a 360-degree view of your ecosystem so that current and potential threats can be identified, analyzed, and dealt with before they even have a chance to fully develop?

As in the previous restaurant and paperwork examples, it's easy to get focused on what you're doing and lose sight of what's around you. You may even *think* you're keeping sight of what's around you, while you're only looking at what's ahead of you or what's behind you.

Getting wrapped up in our own comfortable moments (like eating a meal or sitting in a patrol car) can allow us to easily slip into a mode where we ignore dimensions. The distraction provided by the task at hand can encourage us to simplify what we see around us.

In the car example, if you're parked on the side of a road, you may only be looking at what's ahead of you and the cars coming up behind you. But how about the person who may be approaching your back passenger door?

What's the equivalent of a back passenger door in your business, category, industry, or family/home life? Where are the blind spots?

Whose responsibility is it to see them before they become a problem? The reality is you need to designate someone to have responsibility for that role. If someone isn't tasked specifically with identifying threats, you'll most certainly miss at least some.

COMMUNICATE THE THREATS AND PLAN YOUR RESPONSES

Once you identify the threats, the next challenge is to communicate these threats (both current and potential) to the organization. Do you have a process? Are identified threats buried in long weekly meetings or even in lengthy emails that aren't read? Finding the threats is not enough. People need to know about them in time to react to them and defeat them.

We have detectives whose job is to identify and communicate potential officer safety threats. They uncover the people who are most likely to become issues and develop intelligence on them. They then communicate those threats to the department via official documentation. Teams then discuss those threats and ensure everyone is aware of them and of the implications in our day-to-day jobs. Hazard hits are logged in the computer system and tagged to the people who are potential threats, their vehicles, and their known residences. The legitimacy and value of this work is reinforced at all levels. As a result, reactions are pre-planned and understood.

Speaking of reacting, how much time and energy do you spend planning potential responses to threats such as these? Just like the restaurant, you don't want to wait until the crisis is upon you to determine how you'll respond. You must do your scenario planning ahead of time, and make sure everyone on the team is aware so you can act and aggressively attack threats in real time.

Then you need to document those plans and practice them. In law enforcement, we do scenario training. If we're working on our response to an active shooter in a school, we'll do a day of training with Simunition (think paintballs, but they hurt more), using actors to play students, teachers, and shooters. How does it feel to walk past an injured victim who is pleading for help while you try to get to and eliminate the threat to make it safe for a medical team to reach them? It's difficult and heart wrenching and goes completely against our human nature.

That's why we must practice it. We have actors whose job is to play the role of injured victims, yelling and cursing at us to help them as we move past with the mission of eliminating the threat, so that if we ever have to deal with the real thing, we already know what we're going to do.

How can you set up realistic scenario training in your business? Can you set up a simulated crisis and work through how each person should respond? Sure, you can. You can set up a training day where some worst-case scenarios are played out, and you can practice how you'd handle them.

Say you work for a food company. What do you do if someone tampered with your product and you walked into work to find out that people are getting sick? You now have a lot of people who need to do a lot of things very quickly. People's safety and health are on the line. Beyond that, your company's reputation and ability to bounce back will be dictated by how you react in the minutes and hours that follow. Who's in charge? What does each division and team need to do? How is it all coordinated? This is not the type of thing you want everyone figuring out on their own in the moment, so you practice it, all together, making it as real as possible. And you make mistakes—so you don't make them when it counts.

THE ROAD RUNNER EFFECT

A common error you might make when evaluating threats is to become so focused on a single enemy or a defined set of enemies, dangers, or threats that you form tunnel vision. You become so familiar with that enemy or threat that you can miss other dangers that are lurking in your blind spots. I call this the Road Runner effect.

Wile E. Coyote and the Road Runner are Looney Tunes cartoon characters with a long-standing rivalry. Wile E. Coyote's singular purpose focuses on trying to catch the Road Runner by using absurdly complex schemes. He focuses so much so that he often fails to see the other dangers developing around him (most of which he created in the first place).

It can be the same with your competitors. You become so accustomed to who your company's competitive set is that everything you do is with them in mind. But the more comfortable you become with the threats *you know*, the more vulnerable you become to the ones *you don't*.

If you feel confident that you can rattle off your four biggest competitors and what they're up to, you may want to take a step back and ask yourself what you might be missing. It's a version of survivorship bias—you've been successful to date by focusing on your big competitors. That success can lead you to believe that these are the only ones that matter.

The first step to addressing these issues that arise from the Road Runner effect is to understand that the blind spots exist and then formalize an approach to ensuring the discovery and elimination of those blind spots. If you're doing a competitive analysis or landscape, ensure you always include a spot for the unknown, and make sure someone has responsibility for spending time identifying who may be in that unknown category—now and in the future.

You can see from the examples in this chapter that there is a lot that can be learned from the ways law enforcement maintains threat visibility and scenario planning for success. In summary:

1. Keep the threats in sight.

2. Actively identify where new threats may appear and get eyes on them.

3. Plan responses to threats well before they ever appear.

4. Beware of the Road Runner effect.

CHAPTER THREE VIGILANCE CHECK

Ask yourself:

1. What are the worst-case scenarios for your business? For your home life?

2. Where could the warning signals come from? What is your equivalent of the exits and windows in a restaurant?

3. How can you keep eyes on those areas of vulnerability so that you can identify the threats early? How can you set up so that you maintain a 360-degree view of potential threats?

4. What are some scenarios that you can formulate a plan for *now*? Remember that the worst time to plan for a crisis is

when you are already in it!

5. Who are your Road Runners? How can you expand your definition of your competitors and threats to ensure you're not missing any?

CHAPTER FOUR

Get Off the X: The Advantages of Strategic Unpredictability

I grew up in western Long Island, New York, right next to Queens. Before that, we lived in Brooklyn. My parents were not—how should I put it?—outdoorsy. We didn't fish, camp, hike, or really do anything that involved nature. And we certainly didn't hunt or own guns.

So, when I started the police academy, I didn't have any experience in firearms or shooting. That worked out fine, as I learned everything from scratch the police way.

One of the things that we were constantly browbeaten about was the idea of "get off the X!" What this means is, don't stand still. Imagine you're standing on a big painted X on the ground. Now, *get off it!*

Don't stay where your enemy expects you to be. Draw your weapon and step left or right. Need to reload? Take a step, reload, and then step again when you're ready to put your weapon back on target.

If you're ever at a gun range, you'll be able to instantly tell the difference between a law enforcement officer and a civilian. One will be standing still and popping off rounds. The other will be moving, side to side, getting off the X. But why?

Inevitably, when we'd discuss getting off the X, we'd also talk about disrupting the OODA loop. This is the concept behind getting off the X. I think you'll find that it's incredibly useful in business and in life.

The concept of the OODA (rhymes with Gouda) loop was created by Colonel John Boyd of the United States Air Force. Colonel Boyd flew during the Korean War, wrote tactics for the USAF Weapons School, and later served in the Pentagon doing mathematical analysis. But he really made a name for himself as an influential military strategist.

The OODA loop was Colonel Boyd's model for explaining decision-making and was first used to better understand how fighter pilots could more consistently win their dogfights by being more agile than their opponents. It was delivered as part of his "Patterns of Conflict" briefing. It was about "how to create menace and uncertainty and distrust, then how to exploit and magnify the presence of these disconcerting elements," leading to the "unravelling [of] the competition."[16] Agility, to Colonel Boyd, was more important than technology or strength.

The applications for you are extensive.

OODA is, as you've probably deduced, an acronym. So, let's first break down what the OODA loop stands for:

Observe–Orient–Decide–Act

The first step of the OODA loop is built around *observation*. This is where we collect all the raw information, data, and stimuli from the outside environment. It informs all the other steps.

We're constantly doing this at work. Whether it's reading or watching the news in our industry, going through our emails, visiting and checking in on stores or clients, we're constantly observing—collecting raw information from a wide array of inputs.

Then, we *orient* ourselves. We process and filter the information we've gathered. We compare with previous experiences. We interpret based on culture, expectations, environment, etc., and develop or redevelop a perspective. We have meetings, we discuss, we prepare reports, we crunch numbers, we present. Still, a lot of the orientation may happen in our heads, especially when we have lots of experience and history to compare the new information with. This orientation is what gives our observations meaning.

Part of this orientation stage is formulating potential courses of action in response to the new understanding of this new information.

We then *decide*, choosing the optimal path forward. We gain consensus, getting everybody on board and in agreement.

And finally, we *act*, thereby executing along that decided path (i.e., we execute the plans that everyone at work has given approval for).

It's important to note that the OODA loop isn't a continuous linear process. Feedback is gained each step of the way. When the feedback implies that something has changed that may alter the relevance and applicability of any of the previous steps, the mind begins the process again. For example, if you decide to make a left turn at a stop sign, but then notice another car coming at a speed that makes it unlikely they'll be able to stop, you'll abort the action and start your decision process all over. You reobserve, reorient, and redecide before you finally act.

At work, perhaps you've decided to make a price change on a key product line, but you've just received some new sales information from the previous week that shows a significant strategic shift from one of your major competitors. At this point, you may pull the cord on the planned course of action and re-meet, re-crunch the numbers, loop in some new players, and come to a new consensus before acting.

THE OODA LOOP IS SOMETHING TO BE WON

While the left turn or pricing change examples above were a bit reactionary, the real power in understanding the OODA loop lies in your ability to use it proactively. To stay on your front foot. To control the action.

In business, just like in the military, sports, and law enforcement, the OODA loop is something *to be won*.

In "Tribute to John R. Boyd," published in the July 1997 issue of *Code One* magazine, Harry Hillaker, a colleague of Boyd's and the designer of the F-16, explained that the key of the OODA loop is to hide what your intentions are (and make yourself unpredictable) while you're also clarifying your opponents' intentions.[17] By acting faster and creating a constantly changing environment, you make it harder for your opponent to keep up, thereby confusing them and slowing them down even more.

Hillaker goes on to assert that time is the deciding factor in winning the OODA loop. The one who gets through the loop fastest can appear the most unpredictable, making their opponent react to old information and, ultimately, make a mistake.

So, essentially, there are two ways you can leverage the OODA loop to win versus your competitors:

1. Disrupt (and slow down) your competitor's OODA loop through unpredictability.

2. Speed up your own OODA loop.

While they're both equally important, the first point is the one that's far more applicable to the concept of fighting complacency. So, for the remainder of this chapter we'll focus on how to get off the X and disrupt the competition's OODA loop.

MAKE THE COMPETITION BREAK THEIR ANKLES (FIGURATIVELY)

At the core of the OODA loop is decision-making based on determined observations and orientation. The more things stay static, in that there's no need to reobserve or reorient, the more the process remains linear, and the quicker we can get to the decision phase.

For example, think about a game of football. If your opponent is running with the ball straight down the field, your mind can easily plot a path that gets you to them before they reach the end zone. The math is simple, and it becomes about just pure speed and strength. You observe what the opponent is doing. You orient yourself based on your analysis of their movements, direction, speed, objective, etc. You decide where you're going, and you act on that immediately.

Now let's complicate the matter. In this new scenario, the opponent doesn't run in a straight line. Say they make a stutter step one way or another or make a sharp cut. The observations are changing by the microsecond. With each juke, your mind now must restart the OODA loop. You've observed something different than expected, and now you must reorient before deciding the path to take.

The sheer fact that you're forced to react to your opponent's decision puts you at a disadvantage. The more the information you're receiving is different than what you expected, the more time it takes you to process it and redetermine the correct decision (much less act on it).

Think about the pricing decision example used previously. We were about to make a move. We had done all the data gathering, analysis, and consensus-building, and we had decided. But right at the last minute, we got new information about a preemptive move our main competitor had taken, and it forced us to go back to the start. We had to then reevaluate, taking into consideration this new data. And what does that do, especially in a corporate environment with lots of decision-making layers and people who need to be consulted and appeased? It takes time. It slows us down.

This idea of making the competition react to constantly changing information is how a football punt returner can make the defense fall flat on their faces. It's how a basketball player can make their defender look silly while they end up sinking a wide-open shot. It's why there are so many ankle-breaker YouTube videos for football, basketball, and soccer.

An ankle-breaker is when someone changes direction so quickly and unexpectedly that it causes the defending player to fall over. It's the ultimate in-your-face move and it's usually destined for a highlight reel, etching the humiliating moment in history. Translating it to the OODA loop, the defender has received the visual information and oriented themselves based on their experience and analysis of the inputs. They're so sure of where the offensive player is going or what they're going to do that they decide and act—only to receive new information at the last moment. They try desperately to work through the OODA loop again with the new information, but it's too late. The attempt to change direction is overridden by the body's existing momentum. The defender is unable to stay on their feet and ends up falling to the ground in an awkward mess as the player glides past in triumph.

In law enforcement (as in life in general), we're not looking to humiliate anyone. But just as in sport and in business, when we *move*, we force our enemy to restart their OODA loop. When we put ourselves somewhere different than they expected, when we change the inputs, they have to reorient, which slows them down, makes their responses ineffective, and may provide us the time we need to win the fight (whatever the fight may be).

When we don't move (i.e., don't get off the X), or when we move predictably, we inherently put ourselves at risk. Think about that punt returner. If they stand still and just catch the ball, they're a sitting duck. There's a whole rule (fair catch) in place to protect that punt returner who is standing on the X. Otherwise, they'd most certainly get seriously injured.

The same risk exists for you and your organization, and, unfortunately, your competitors are probably not going to abide by a fair catch rule.

The problem is that the path of least resistance is predictable. It's easy, and most of the time it probably works out just fine (survivorship bias). But it can lead to your unwittingly putting yourself in danger from your opponent or even yourself.

The goal is to constantly be thinking about how you can get off the X. How can you disrupt your competitors' thinking to force them to be slower to act? How can you introduce new and unexpected information that sends them back to the start of their OODA loop over and over? How can you be strategically unpredictable?

BUILDING UNPREDICTABILITY INTO YOUR PROCESS

Let's be clear. The objective is not to be wild or unstructured. But you can build intentional unpredictability into your strategy.

Professional poker players do this to win. While an amateur may always bet big and go all in when they get pocket aces, the pro will break up their strategy to remain unpredictable. Seventy percent of the time they may lead in with a big bet. But 30 percent of the time, they may play their aces like they're holding nothing at all.

As famous poker pro Daniel Negreanu puts it, "If you never limp in with aces, you might as well put a target on your forehead whenever you do limp into a pot. It will become apparent to your opponents that when you limp in before the flop, you probably don't have a big pair. That's revealing too much information. You'd be playing too predictably."[18]

The bonus of playing poker (or running your business) this way is that you can *appear* to be unstructured, while remaining quite the opposite. In fact, the *appearance* of unpredictability is often enough to slow your opponent down. Just the idea that what they're observing may not be reality forces them to consider more options and take more time in the orientation phase, delaying the time to decision and action.

In law enforcement, we look for ways to remain unpredictable and we build it into our processes. There are many examples that go beyond our use of movement when drawing and using our weapons.

When I approach a car that I've pulled over for a traffic violation, I can approach it from the driver's side or from the passenger's side. I may even stay back at my car and ask the driver to step out and come back to me. Sometimes there'll be a reason. Sometimes it'll be purely random. If I always go to the driver's side door, I become predictable. By switching it up, I get off the X.

We build in unpredictability in other ways as well. We change up the entry and exit points when patrolling a neighborhood, for example. If I'm working a special assignment that requires visiting a set group of schools, I'll change up the order in which I visit them each time. I'll also take different routes home after a shift just to make sure no one can predict my route and no one's following me.

In sports, as we've already seen, it can all be a bit more…dramatic.

In 2010, the New Orleans Saints were trailing the Indianapolis Colts by a score of 10–6 at halftime. The Saints were set to kick off to start the second half when they pulled off what ESPN sportswriter Mike Triplett later called "the NFL's gutsiest play call," an onside kick.[19]

An onside kick is a play where, during a kickoff, the kicker squib-kicks the ball instead of kicking it long. The goal is to get it to bounce erratically until it goes at least 10 yards and then pops up into the air. If it goes 10 yards, the kicking team is eligible to recover the ball without the receiving team ever touching it. Oftentimes, when it works, the receiving team does touch it, but the weirdly rotating ball proves hard to handle, especially with a bunch of 300-pound players running full speed into you as you leap in the air.

The reality, though, is that an onside kick rarely works. It's mostly used as a last resort at the end of a game. Most of the time, the receiving team knows exactly what's happening and they're ready for it. They put their most reliable receivers in the front and are prepared for what's coming.

When it doesn't work, the receiving team gets fantastic field position. All in all, it's a play with a traditionally low probability of success. It's almost *never* used to start a half, and used even less to start a half in a close game during a Super Bowl, which is what made this call by Saint's head coach Sean Payton so remarkable. He knew the up players on the Colts would never be expecting an onside kick. They'd be so sure a regular kickoff was coming that they'd be on their heels and running back almost before the kick was taken.

And, so, when that unpredictable kick came, the Colts were very much not ready for it. And it worked. The Saints got the ball, and they ended up winning their only Super Bowl.

You can also bet that since then, coaches and players alike have always considered, somewhere in their minds, the possibility of something unpredictable coming from Coach Payton. I mean, if he was willing to do that during a close Super Bowl, what's he capable of when the situation is less monumental? Maybe that means the receiving team has to be a little more flat-footed. They must be ready for the possibility of the unpredictable, even if it never comes.

Without a doubt, though, being predictable is easier. It requires less thought. Eat at the same place at the same time every night. Approach every traffic stop the same way. Go on autopilot on the way home. Execute a kickoff the same way every time.

Maybe even be so predictable that you train your most loyal customers to work against you.

RETAIL PREDICTABILITY

I'm not what you would call fashion-forward. Utilitarian is probably a better description of how I prefer to dress. I like pants with lots of pockets. Zippers and Velcro are always welcome. I like shirts that are comfortable and travel well. I like Eddie Bauer.

Over the course of a year, I shop EddieBauer.com several times. I don't love going into stores, and I know how their stuff fits me. Their clothes are not super expensive, so, at first, I didn't pay much attention to their sales. If I needed something, I bought it. If it happened to be on sale, great!

But then, it seems a few years ago, I started getting very frequent emails about Eddie Bauer sales. It seemed like there was one every week. The discounts would range from 30 percent off to 50 percent or even 60 percent off! It became quickly apparent that buying anything from Eddie Bauer at full price was incredibly foolish. In fact, buying anything at less than 50 percent off felt like paying a premium.

The more I paid attention, the more I realized that the best sales always came at predictable times—obviously at Christmas, but also on President's Day, Memorial Day, Independence Day, Labor Day, etc. Once I figured out there were enough predictable time periods where the discounts would be *at least* 50 percent off, I stopped paying attention to anything less.

Thirty percent off became as foolish as full price. Why would I pay that when 50 to 60 percent off was just around the corner? Eddie Bauer is standing firmly on the X. I know it. I am sure their competition knows it. They even probably know it. So, why would they do this?

They do it because it's easier. It's the way they've always done it. The previous year's numbers they are trying to hit are tied to those offers. If they move them, they may fear they'll miss key numbers on key dates. They've locked themselves into a vicious cycle that they can't get out of. Well, they probably could, but it would be painful in the short term.

Sometimes, though, that short-term pain is required to bring a bit of the mystery back to the process. If you keep doing things the same way, you never force anyone to reconsider the inputs to their OODA loop. And eventually, it'll catch up with you.

Eddie Bauer has had a tumultuous last decade. After emerging from bankruptcy, they were purchased by a private equity firm. Subsequently, they were combined with Pacific Sunwear to create the operating company PSEB. In 2018, an article written about the merging of the two companies suggested that part of the reason for the merger was to help "solve Golden Gate's ongoing problem of unloading Eddie Bauer. The brand spent most of the 21st century burdened with debt, surviving two trips to bankruptcy court." The author also pointed out that Eddie Bauer needed to show strong holiday sales to avoid seeing its rating lowered further, having already been on a list of stores at risk of bankruptcy.[20]

Remember that the antidote for predictability for our purposes here isn't just haphazard unpredictability. The answer is *strategic unpredictability*. This requires forethought and intentional action. It's harder than being predictable, but the rewards can be significant in terms of slowing down your opponent's OODA loop and buying you the precious time you need to win.

FORCE YOURSELF OFF THE X THROUGH SELF-DISRUPTION

According to past Brand ManageCamp marketing conference speaker Soren Kaplan (best-selling author of *Leapfrogging* and *The Invisible Advantage* and an affiliate at the Center for Effective Organizations at USC's Marshall School of Business), we have two choices—disrupt or be disrupted. One involves a proactive stance, and the other, reactive. Your choice on this matter also dictates where your competition will be. If you choose to actively disrupt your brand and your category, you'll force your competitor to reobserve and reorient. You'll no longer be standing where they expected you to be. You'll be off the X. You may have even moved the X altogether.

Netflix was once a DVD rental service that sent you movies in a returnable envelope. When it was founded in 1998, this idea was a disruption to the traditional bricks-and-mortar video stores like Blockbuster. Later, it disrupted itself (and forever changed the industry, leaving the original players in their dust) by moving its business predominantly to streaming services. It then disrupted itself again by moving into the world of content production. Love it or hate it, there is no denying that *Tiger King* was a commercial success, being watched by 34.3 million unique viewers in the first 10 days of its release (according to Nielsen).[21]

Since its start, Netflix has committed itself to disrupting its industry and its own business models—always staying a step ahead of its competitors. Because it's always a moving target, it's hard to catch.

FROM ACADEMIC PAPERS TO INSTAGRAM SUCCESS

National Geographic magazine was first published in 1888, shortly after the founding of the National Geographic Society. The society itself was founded with a mission to "increase and diffuse geographic knowledge."[22] For decades, it was a mainstay on coffee tables around the globe with its trademark beautiful nature photography. But, when the magazine first started, it didn't have that photography; it was filled with academic papers.

When Alexander Graham Bell became president of the company, a plan was hatched to evolve by bringing stories to people through pictures. The first photograph (a relief map of North America) was printed in a *National Geographic* issue in 1889, and the first natural-color photograph showed up in 1914, setting it apart from the rest of the competition.[23]

Over time, this photography was no longer unique to *National Geographic*. Although it was successful, it was still looking for ways to stand out. In the 1960s, it started to produce programming for CBS television in the United Sates. Though it was educational and academic, it took the stories off the pages of a magazine and created a new medium to connect with its consumers. Stars like Jacques Cousteau and Jane Goodall were born.

In the 1990s, *National Geographic* magazine experienced the same declines and issues common in the print industry, and ad dollars were disappearing. Its circulation dropped in the 2000s to half of what it had been in the 1980s. The brand seemed old and stale, and those were not good qualities in an industry that was already troubled.

That's when it decided to make the move into cable television with its own network (in conjunction with Rupert Murdoch's Fox media network). It was now beamed into hundreds of millions of homes in nearly 200 countries. It was bringing in much needed revenue, making up for declines in magazine ad sales and membership subscriptions. While the other magazines were trying to compete for a dwindling number of readers, *National Geographic* changed the rules and found another way to succeed.[24]

But it didn't stop there. Around 2012, the folks at National Geographic were looking for ways to connect with a younger audience and stay relevant. With its history firmly entrenched in amazing photography, Instagram was an obvious choice. Since then, National Geographic has become a stunning Instagram success story. As of this writing, its Instagram account has over 135 million followers. That puts it at number 11 of *all Instagram accounts*, edging out many of the world's biggest celebrities and social media influencers.[25]

Repeatedly, National Geographic has disrupted itself to stay ahead of the competition. And through it all, it has remained true to its original vision.

MOVING THE X BY MOVING PERSONNEL

At the Douglas County Sheriff's Office, we break our county down into 12 districts. We use these districts to assign patrol deputies to areas of responsibility. When you work a district for an extended period, you become familiar with the geography, the businesses, the schools, the people, and the traffic. You learn patterns and schedules. You build relationships.

But you can also become predictable. You can form your own patterns. Going to the same place for food. Making a stop at the same time each day to talk with a clerk at a specific convenience store. Dropping by the same schools to see the kids and interact as they arrive or leave.

The familiarity can become a double-edged sword. While it's important to have those relationships and that deep understanding of your territory, it can also lead to you getting off the X less and less frequently.

So, our sergeants switch things up. Each one has a different schedule they like to follow. Some change assignments every few weeks. For others it may be four times a year. Regardless, there's a predetermined, built-in personnel shuffle that forces them to literally get off the X. It's a forced disruption.

You can, and should, do this in business, too. When I worked for Campbell Soup and Coca-Cola, a trademark for the marketing teams was that employees didn't stay in their roles for very long. Anybody who was kept in their exact role for a period of any more than one or two years appeared stagnant in comparison to their peers. So even if employees weren't moving up in title, they were moved to a new brand or a new category.

This has a dual purpose. First, it keeps the employees on their toes and forces them to constantly learn and adapt their learnings to new environments. This keeps them fresh and engaged, as marketers tend to be type-A people who can get bored quickly. Second, it helps the thinking on the brands stay fresh and evolving. As new people rotate in, status quos are questioned. New ideas are brought in. New directions are explored. According to the May 30, 2019, *Forbes* article, "Talent Mobility: The Key To Unlocking Your Organization's Potential," by Rebecca Skilbeck, talent "mobility provides avenues for staff to progress and evolve within an organization and can lead to 30% better processes and 23% more productivity."[26]

This doesn't happen because the new people are smarter than the others. They're just different. And that difference leads to different thinking and helps to combat predictability. It gets the brands off the X. And, hopefully, it keeps the competition guessing.

BALANCE IS THE KEY

Keep in mind, the purpose of doing all these things—both at work and at home—is to remain unpredictable *in a strategic way*. You must balance all of this with a constant eye towards your customer, consumer, or partner. The risk is that too much nonstrategic unpredictability could create a less than ideal brand experience for them. To revisit the football analogy, the player with the ball is still, predictably, trying to make their way to the end zone. They're just, ideally, doing it in a way that disrupts their opponent's OODA loop.

Of course, there are plenty of times when predictability is important. You don't want your customer to be guessing what their experience is going to be each time they interact with you. The key is to understand what the core of that desired experience is and to deliver it consistently even while you're moving off the X or disrupting yourself or your industry.

Done correctly, embracing the concept of moving off the X, disrupting your competitor's OODA loop, and remaining strategically unpredictable can tilt the odds of success in your favor while also keeping things interesting for all involved.

CHAPTER FOUR VIGILANCE CHECK

Ask yourself:

1. Where are you most predictable? Which elements of that predictability could be vulnerabilities?

2. What are opportunities for you to get off the X?

3. Where is outside disruption most likely to come from? How can you preemptively disrupt yourself so that you can control the outcome?

4. Who on your team at work could benefit from a change of role or responsibilities? How can you create an opportunity for a shuffle?

CHAPTER FIVE

———

Briefing and Debriefing: Question Everything, Even When Everything Goes Right

Recently I was working a day shift in the northwest part of our county. There's no typical day in law enforcement, and you quickly learn that anything can, and will, happen at any given time of day. In general, though, day shifts are heavier on cold crimes than they are on in-progress crimes.

Cold crimes are ones that have already happened. For example, you wake up and go to the garage, and realize it's open and all your tools are gone. Or someone has trespassed into your vehicle. Or you realize you're missing a credit card and it has charges on it. In worst-case scenarios, you discover a person who has died overnight of natural causes.

These are not unimportant crimes; they're just not the high-stress, lights-and-sirens type of calls. Again, the high-stress calls do happen on day shift, just not as frequently.

So, when the call came out over the radio that there were shots fired in a residential neighborhood in broad daylight, the response was quick and broad. Police cars started moving towards the call, with lights and sirens, immediately. The first cars went right to the threat. Secondary responding cars began to set up a perimeter. Those of us not needed on the perimeter donned rifle protection, deployed our long guns, and started getting put into position in key locations by the on-site command.

The information we received was that the shooter had retreated into a house and was alone. We surrounded the location, keeping eyes on all sides. SWAT came in and made announcements. After several hours, SWAT entered the house and discovered the shooter had taken his own life.

From most perspectives, we did everything correctly. No innocent citizens were hurt, no deputies were injured, and the situation was concluded without our firing a single shot.

The scope of this call took many deputies off the street. It took an enormous amount of manpower to respond, set up a perimeter, and maintain scene security until the call was completed.

It may seem that the first thought of command staff, once everything was deemed safe on scene, would be to get everyone back to their districts and back to work. But no.

The command came out over the radio: Everyone who had been on this call was to rendezvous in the briefing room at our substation within the next half hour. Once everyone was assembled, the sergeant who'd been running command began our debriefing.

We went through the entire call. We talked about what went right. We talked about what went wrong. We talked about what went right by accident or even despite mistakes we had made. We talked about what we would do differently.

We went around the room and every person—from the top brass to the deputy who was still in field training—was given an opportunity to speak and raise issues. Many offered up things they'd seen from their specific viewpoints, good and bad. And we discussed the implications of those for the future.

And *then* we went back to work.

VIGILANCE IS QUESTIONING EVERYTHING, EVEN WHEN EVERYTHING GOES RIGHT

Take note that the debriefing took place while everything was still fresh. It involved everyone without respect to seniority or experience. And it took place after a call where we seemingly did everything correctly.

Maybe you do debriefing in your organization right now. But, if you're like most, you debrief only after perceived failures. This approach is designed to find out *what went wrong* and how to fix it. It's not usually done immediately, and it's probably not an open forum. In fact, the person or people in charge of debriefing have probably already decided what went wrong, and the debriefing may really be for chastising people who made mistakes.

This tendency to focus energy only on debriefing things that were perceived to go wrong is strongly linked back to complacency and survivorship bias. It's why most organizations don't spend time on debriefing things that go right. Success is usually seen as self-explanatory. I mean, if the results were positive, we must've done things right. Right?

Wrong. We frequently get positive results from less-than-optimal performances (remember survivorship bias?). Professional athletes understand this. Professional football players spend hours a day watching game film during each week of preparation in addition to the physical practicing. Most of this time is spent watching footage of their upcoming opponent. They study their offenses and defenses to the point that, come game time, there are virtually no surprises to be had.

Before all of that, they spend two to three hours on Monday (assuming they played on Sunday) studying the film from their own game the day before. They break down their own play in the game and look for mistakes. They look for mental errors, breakdowns in technique, and anything that can be improved upon.

And *they don't just do this when they lose*. They understand that, even in victory, there are things that can be improved. They understand that just because they had more points than their competition, it doesn't mean they did everything right, not by a long shot. In fact, they may have played poorly, but the other team just played worse. Or they got a lucky bounce of the ball. Or they got a favorable referee decision. Whatever it is, it doesn't matter that they got the win. They know they still need to look for ways to improve. It's just as important to look for the things that went right so they can identify them and figure out how to create situations that make it more likely that those things will happen again.

NFL Hall of Fame quarterback Peyton Manning is famous for his dedication to game study.[27] If he only did this when he lost, he would have a lot of Mondays off! But his dedication to debriefing and looking for anything he could do differently has set him apart from the competition.

Clyde Christensen, an Indianapolis Colts wide receiver coach from 2002 to 2008 and offensive coordinator from 2009 to 2011, recounted this story in an October 4, 2017, article in the IndyStar:

> *I'd be asleep on the plane ride home coming back from a road win, sometimes at 1, 2 in the morning, and the stewardess would come tap me on the shoulder. "Peyton wants to see you in the back of the plane." I'd tell her to tell him I was sleeping. She'd come back a few minutes later. "He said he doesn't care if you're sleeping." So, I'd walk back there, and we'd go over the entire game, play after play after play. He loved everything there was to football. He noticed every detail.*[28]

Many times, when you hear an announcer lament about a team's complacency during a game, this can be traced back to a lack of preparation in the time leading up to the game. Success has a way of creating a lull, a sense of self-satisfaction, and overconfidence. Overconfident is a description you would never hear used for Peyton Manning, Tom Brady, or most other Hall of Fame–worthy athletes. They dissect success ad nauseam. And it's why they deliver consistently positive results.

Debriefing is also utilized religiously in the military. Lt. Col. Waldo Waldman is a graduate of the Air Force Academy, a decorated fighter pilot, and the best-selling author of *Never Fly Solo*. Waldman, in one of his videos about being mission-ready, says:

> *The one thing fighter pilots do after every mission is, we debrief... When fighter pilots come back from combat and training*

missions, we do something sacred - we have a debriefing.
We get into a room, and for an hour, and perhaps three to
four hours, we sit down and learn from the mission.[29]

The medical world started to embrace debriefing in the context of learning from simulations they ran. However, the practice is now widely accepted and used in relation to actual clinical events as well. On its Patient Safety Network, the Agency for Healthcare Research and Quality states:

Although real-time or near real-time clinical event debriefing
can be challenging to implement, it has been identified as
an important aspect of effective clinical education, quality
improvement, and systems learning. It is important to note that
debriefing can be a useful learning tool in cases where things go
well, with near misses, and in cases that involve adverse events.[30]

HOW TO BE SUCCESSFUL WITH DEBRIEFING

Based on learnings from law enforcement, military, sports, and healthcare, here are seven ways you can be more successful with debriefing.

1. **Understand your missions and find opportunities to debrief.**

   Police have individual calls, cases, or critical incidents to debrief. Fighter pilots have distinct missions. Football players have games. Medical professionals have clinical events. What do you have to debrief?

It's important to be able to break your business down into your own distinct missions. You must be able to identify starting and end points. You need to understand what the objectives were for each mission. It could be the development of an advertisement, a sales meeting, a holiday promotion, or the development and delivery of an internal report. Whatever the distinct events are, you must identify them in order to debrief them.

2. **Don't make debriefing dependent on outcome.**

We've already discussed the tendency in the corporate world to debrief only the things that appeared to go wrong. As we've seen from the previous examples, though, successful debriefing can take place regardless of whether the results were positive or negative.

Sometimes the greatest learning comes from the incidents that were perceived as the most successful. Often, it's in those moments—the ones spent reflecting on the drivers of and potential missteps in perceived successes—that the true battle against complacency is fought. This is truly where vigilance prevails.

3. **Debrief frequently and as close to the incident as possible.**

Debrief in a timely manner. Utilize video or audio conferencing if everyone is in different places. Do whatever you need to do to make the debriefings happen as close to the event as possible, because you'll want people's fresh reactions.

People should understand and expect that these debriefings will take place. Make them muscle memory, not just random events. When people know they'll have an opportunity to discuss how things went afterward, they'll inevitably pay more attention to what's going on around them. They'll have more observations and be more prepared with thoughts, knowing that they'll have a forum where they can voice them.

4. **Leave titles and ranks outside.**

   It's important to leave titles out of the equation when it comes to debriefing. No one's opinion is worth more or less than anyone else's. Everyone gets a say—from the top level on the team to the newest member. This is the only way everyone will feel comfortable enough to share.

   You may even find that the newest team members will often be the ones to find the areas of improvement that everyone else has become blind to. They aren't burdened with the weight of the status quo. They have fresh eyes and ideas. Don't inhibit them.

5. **Be clear on mission objectives.**

   While the decision to hold a debriefing shouldn't be predicated on success or failure, it's important to know which one you've had. You need to understand desired processes and outcomes to understand how well you fared against them.

6. **Incorporate structure into the meeting.**

   During debriefing, it can be easy to get bogged down in what happened, why it happened, whose fault it was, etc. It's important to make sure you get past that. Of course, you should start with the "what." But make sure you have a structure in place that allows you to then move to two other critical components, "So what?" and "Now what?"

"So what?" focuses on which elements of the "what" are the most important. Which elements have the greatest implications and deserve the most scrutiny? A lot of feedback can come out in the debriefing. It's important to be able to separate out the elements that require attention from the others.

The last question is, "Now what?" The whole process is useless if it's not used to drive future behavior. What are you going to keep doing? What are you going to do differently? How will you make sure?

7. **Share the findings broadly.**

The information collected during debriefing is not just for your team, your project, or your incident. Make sure the findings are shared more broadly to ensure everyone in the organization can learn and benefit.

REGULAR BRIEFINGS ARE JUST AS IMPORTANT

The flip side of the debriefing session is the briefing session. Of the two, this is the one that you should do more regularly, as it's not based on a project or mission completion. In law enforcement, this is something we do before every shift.

At the start of every shift, our team members get together in a single room (or, in our case, two different locations tied together by a video call). The sergeant goes through emails that have come out. We discuss incidents that have happened since our last shift that are important for us to know. Are there any hotspots we need to be aware of? Are there any addresses that had incidents that could flare back up? Really, we discuss anything else we need to be aware of to do our jobs as safely and effectively as possible. On the 1980s TV show *Hill Street Blues*, every one of their briefings ended with Sergeant Esterhaus saying, "Let's be careful out there."[31]

Briefings are also used to debrief noncritical events from the previous shift. It may include a specific call that generated some useful talking points. Not everything is big enough to justify a debriefing.

Also, briefings are an opportunity for team members to share things they may be working on. It could involve a follow-up they may need help with, or things they are seeing in their districts that could affect others.

Another thing we accomplish in briefings is what we call Seven Minute Trainings. Each day, one member of the shift is responsible for a training topic. It can be anything they want—a new court ruling that has implications for us, a video of a critical incident from another department that we can critique and discuss, or a new or changed internal policy to be explained. It doesn't have to end at exactly the seven minute mark, but it's an opportunity to ensure we are constantly looking for ways to learn and become better and, ultimately, safer in our jobs.

Finally, briefings are the one opportunity we may have during a shift when everyone is together. We might see a few other deputies on calls that require more than one of us. But most deputies won't see each other again until the shift is over, if even then. So, these briefings are as much about team building and camaraderie as about anything else. There's no shortage of ribbing and kidding and just having a little fun with each other. This part is as important as any other.

The idea of a briefing is likely not foreign to you. You probably already have regular or semiregular team meetings. Or maybe you do one-on-ones with your boss. They are critical in avoiding complacency, because they force us to process new information, to be reminded of potential dangers or threats, to use other people's learnings to help us form new perspectives and levels of understanding, and to avoid the status quo.

MAKING BRIEFINGS BETTER

Here are five things I've learned from our law enforcement briefings that can help make yours more productive.

1. **Do them on a regular schedule, and keep them as short as possible.**

   Our briefings happen whether we think we need them or not. Of course, there's always the pressure to get out on the road quicker. The shift before us is ending, and it's not fair to let them pick up calls that could end up keeping them late. But, outside of extenuating circumstances, the briefing always happens. At the start of *every single shift.* They don't often last long; they usually go anywhere from 10 minutes to 30 minutes. But they happen.

   In the corporate setting, briefings generally don't happen often enough. And when they do happen, they often run too long. Maybe you have a weekly meeting, and it goes an hour in length. You would be much better off doing 15 minutes to start every day. Things move too quickly these days to wait a whole week between briefings. You'll likely even find that you save time by doing the meetings more often. By getting everyone together in the same room (or on the phone or a video call), you can clear up issues and get questions answered more efficiently than trying to track down individuals through-out the day.

2. **Don't cancel them.**

   Do your briefings (or one-on-ones or team meetings) often get cancelled or postponed because something else comes up? If you're like most, your answer is "all the time."

   Listen, I get it. You have a weekly team status meeting first thing Monday. Over the weekend, your boss gets an urgent request from their boss. It's all hands on deck to get this info to the higher-ups. What gives? The status meeting, of course. And then it doesn't get rescheduled because no one can sync their calendars with anyone else's. So, it gets pushed off to the next week.

   Sound familiar? It doesn't seem like too big a deal when it happens, and the circumstances may make it seem like a reasonable sacrifice. Or maybe you don't even look at it as a sacrifice because the meetings are too long and painful.

   This is a slippery slope. And it isn't too long before these meetings, when they actually happen, are just a waste of time. If you suspect they'll often be cancelled, you won't invest your time or energy in properly preparing yourself for them. So, when they do happen, they certainly won't be productive.

3. **Stay focused.**

   Briefings should be used to deliver info critical to the team's success between now and the next briefing. They should allow team members to engage and share their own info critical for the team, and they should incorporate some quick training to keep everyone sharp. If there are bigger issues to discuss, set up a separate meeting that includes only those who are involved. Don't allow regular briefing meetings to get hijacked by other, larger issues. That's just as bad as cancelling them. If you don't respect the importance of the briefing, no one else on the team will either. And then it just becomes a colossal waste of time.

4. **Make sure they're a conversation and not a lecture.**

Make sure everyone across the entire team or family is welcomed to share. If briefings are led by the boss and are just a one-way conversation, they're not true briefings. Everyone should come knowing that they'll have an opportunity to share and that their opinions, questions, concerns, and advice will be valued.

5. **Incorporate a learning element.**

These don't have to be monumental or heavily involved trainings. A great tool for fighting complacency is building in mechanisms to heighten awareness. Perhaps it's a team member sharing an efficiency tool or technique they've developed. Maybe it's a quick case study from another industry or an update on the structure of a key client or even competitor.

Whatever it is, it will stimulate the team members to think about something differently or think about something new they haven't considered before. These are all effective ways to keep the team sharp and less vulnerable to complacency.

BRIEF, DEBRIEF, REPEAT

Law enforcement. Military. Professional sports teams. The medical community. They all enthusiastically embrace the introspection and self-analyzing that comes along with the process of briefing and de-briefing. By taking some of the cues outlined above, you can now use the concepts more consistently and effectively in your business and in your life so that you can continually learn from your failures *and* your successes. This helps in keeping your team members (or family members) actively engaged, aligned, motivated, and vigilant.

CHAPTER FIVE VIGILANCE CHECK

Ask yourself:

1. Think about your recent successes at work and at home. What were things you could have learned from that success if you had debriefed it?

2. Do you currently debrief things that turn out well?

3. How can you incorporate more regular briefings into your work and/or home life?

4. How can you ensure everyone on your team has an equal voice?

CHAPTER SIX

Keep Both Eyes Open: Avoid the Tunnel by Seeing beyond the Target

I was on patrol one summer day when a call came in reporting a potentially drunk driver. The reporting party was behind a vehicle that was swerving and having a hard time maintaining its lane. It appeared that there was a child in a car seat in the back. The car was pulling into a store parking lot.

Armed with the location and a description of the vehicle, I headed to the parking lot. I quickly located the vehicle and determined that it wasn't occupied. My backup arrived, and we decided to wait in the parking lot for the woman and her child to leave the store.

Shortly afterwards, a woman with a child did exit the store and started toward the car. We intercepted her before she arrived at her car to ask some questions and try to determine if she was impaired in any way.

Through our discussion, it was clear that she wasn't under the influence of alcohol. By her description, she was being distracted by her child while she was driving, causing her to swerve a few times. She was apologetic. We looked for signs that she was otherwise impaired, perhaps by drugs. We didn't see any.

The woman then asked if she could put her child in the car, as it was a little chilly out and the child was probably around three to four years old. We were likely letting her go with a warning for distracted driving, so there was no reason to not allow it. As she put the child in the car, I kept an eye on her while talking with the other deputy.

It was then that something caught my eye. The woman appeared to be holding something shiny in her hand. I stepped to the side to get a better look. I could see the shiny object was a silver revolver—and it was pointed at the child.

I immediately drew my firearm, and as I took aim, I yelled at the woman to drop the gun. She was facing inside the car, and when I yelled at her, she began to turn towards me, gun in hand.

As I drew my weapon, in the mere second or two of time that elapsed from then until the episode was over, a lot of things went through my mind. I was trying to make sure she did, in fact, have a weapon. I was mentally deciding which action would prompt me to fire my weapon. I was also taking note of my position relative to the child and what was happening beyond the woman. Was there a family walking behind her? Was there a school bus full of kids driving past? Was there danger of my hitting the child? Was I in any kind of cross-fire situation with my colleague?

About halfway towards squaring up to me, she dropped the gun. As it hit the ground, I immediately realized it was plastic. My gun went back to its holster. I took a deep breath.

My mind had been processing thoughts quickly without me consciously thinking about it. That's where training comes in. We've trained extensively on shoot and no-shoot scenarios. Our minds are conditioned to consider all the implications of discharging our weapons, because we're responsible for every round we throw downrange.

In this scenario, the woman had decided to play toy guns with her child while having a police interaction. Playing with a toy gun with her son was probably a normal thing for her to be doing. She probably didn't give it a second thought—she was just trying to keep the kid occupied and happy.

However, the gun didn't have any of the normal indications of a toy gun (like an orange piece on the end of the barrel). It looked real from afar. This could have gone very badly, very quickly. I (gently) let her know that what she'd just done was…not the smartest idea. She immediately realized her mistake and apologized. I believe the lesson was learned. By both of us.

THE TARGET AND WHAT LIES BEYOND

We could take many complacency lessons from this single encounter if we wanted to unpack the whole thing. We could talk about how important it is to not get lulled into a false sense of security when things seem safe. We could talk about the importance of training and playing out scenarios ahead of time to shorten our OODA loop and increase critical decision-making speed.

But, to me, the main takeaway is the importance of remaining focused while avoiding the tunnel vision that causes you to ignore everything else going on around you. This is the concept of remaining aware of your target in addition to what lies beyond, and it has tremendous relevance far beyond law enforcement.

Complacency can condition us to consider only the target in front of us and to ignore what lies beyond, the implications of the actions, the ripple effects that can be created, and the unintended consequences.

In business, we spend a lot of time defining and refining our target market, right down to even giving our target customers names, faces, and biographies (personas). We can feel like they become part of our family. We know them. We know what's important to them, what drives them, what makes them happy, and what annoys them.

I'm not trying to suggest that this deep understanding of a target market, customer, or consumer is a bad thing. However, it can become a liability if you become so focused on what you've defined as your target that you lose sight of everything else around it. That's where you can miss things such as influencers, environmental changes, and new competition.

In the previous interaction, the woman was focused on entertaining her child. Had she considered how anybody beyond her child (i.e., *the police*!) would interpret her pointing a fake, but real-looking, firearm at her child's face, she most likely would've chosen a different path.

Similarly, I had to consider not just my target (the woman with the perceived gun) but all the other people who could potentially be impacted by my firing a round. Being aware of your target and beyond is a powerful tool to combat situational complacency and avoid unintended consequences.

Smart managers understand they need to be able to manage down *and* up. Smart salespeople know that they need to form relationships not just with their target but with their target's gatekeepers (like their administrative assistants), their influencers, and even their peers in different departments. Smart marketers and advertisers know that their messages will be seen and evaluated by a far wider audience than their narrow target. Failing to understand how those messages will resonate across the spectrum of those seeing them can lead to epic disasters.

It's easy to lose sight of the surroundings, the ancillary players, the influencers, and those that are influenced, and to develop tunnel vision that focuses on the issue at hand and ignores the rest of the ecosystem. To fight this effect of complacency, you first must develop a mindset that's built to include all the information your brain (or organization) wants to ignore.

KEEP BOTH EYES OPEN

It's funny how the same thing can be described two different ways and with two very different connotations. Consider, for example, the terms "laser-focused" and "tunnel vision."

The term "laser-focused" is often used as a compliment. It's a testament to your ability to be so centered on a target or a mission that success is inevitable. It equates to drive and discipline and strength. Focusing a laser gives it more power.

"Tunnel vision," on the other hand, has a negative connotation. It involves being so focused on something that you ignore everything else around it. It's limiting. It omits potentially pertinent information. It can make you unaware of potential risks or dangers. As we discussed in Chapter Three, the Road Runner effect is a type of tunnel vision where you get so focused on a set of competitors that you can't see any of the others coming your way.

So, having tunnel vision really means being laser-focused to the point where you lose sight and awareness of the periphery. There's a fine line between them, and the goal is to not cross it. The key is keeping both eyes open.

THE FOUR RULES OF FIREARM SAFETY

To illustrate this point, I want to first share a simple but powerful lesson we learned on the firing range at academy (and revisit multiple times a year in firearm training). As you might imagine, we spend a lot of time on firearm proficiency. That includes everything from understanding how to clean and maintain our firearms and becoming experts in target acquisition and accuracy, to making the correct shoot or no-shoot decisions in the most stressful situations. While our lessons and exercises may vary, one thing remains the same about any firearms training we have from day one to the end of the watch: gun safety.

There are four basic rules of firearms safety, and no matter how advanced we are, we go over them every time we're on the range. They're the same gun safety rules taught in every firearms class, whether it's law enforcement or civilian. And, regardless of your views on guns or whether you have guns in your house, you should teach these to your children.

1. Treat every gun as if it's loaded.

2. Never point the muzzle at anything you're not willing to destroy.

3. Keep your finger off the trigger and outside of the trigger guard until your sights are on target and you've made the decision to shoot.

4. Be sure of your target and what lies beyond your target.

The fourth rule is the one that has real applicability in fighting complacency in your business and at home. You must be able to avoid the tunnel vision and really see everything that's going on around you. You must maintain a focus on your target, give verbal commands, and move off the X. But if you do all that and lose sight of what's beyond (or around or in front of) your target, it may all be for nothing.

LEARNING TO SHOOT WITH BOTH EYES OPEN

One important skill I learned as I went through firearms training that significantly impacted my ability to see the target and beyond is to shoot with both eyes open. This wasn't a natural thing for me. Remember, I wasn't an experienced shooter when I started the academy. What I knew, I'd seen on TV.

The first time I picked up my handgun and aimed it at a target on the range, I instinctively closed one eye and used only my dominant eye. Closing my nondominant eye was my way of becoming laser-focused on the target, which may not be a bad way of shooting accurately when you're in a controlled, noncombat environment. But it's not ideal out in the real world, because when you close that eye and become laser-focused on the target, you lose the ability to see anything around it. You also lose some depth perception, which has obvious negative repercussions in real life.

Try this exercise. Imagine you're going to take a photograph with a camera, not a phone but an actual camera with a viewfinder that you look through. When you take this picture, you're not going to look at the LCD screen. You're actually going to look through the viewfinder (or, as my daughter would call it, that square thingy you hold up to your eye).

Now, pick up this imaginary camera and choose something across the room or out the window that you want to photograph. Bring the imaginary camera up to your face and look through the imaginary viewfinder. Focus your camera on that object.

If you're like most people, you brought that imaginary camera up to one of your eyes. And what did you do with the other eye? You closed it to allow yourself to get more laser-focused on your subject. But how much attention did you pay to what else was around you while you were doing that?

Now do the exercise again but keep both eyes open this time. Keep your focus on your subject while also remaining aware of what's happening around you. It will feel unnatural, but you should be able to do it just fine. If you have a really hard time doing this, it's likely you're using your nondominant eye to take the photograph. Try switching eyes and see what happens.

Now do it again the original way with one eye closed. You're probably more aware this time of how much you're *not* seeing when you have that eye closed. This is the situational awareness you're losing as a tradeoff for a laser focus on your subject.

If your only objective is to take a picture or hit a target on a firing range, closing one eye may work. But if you must also be concerned with what else is around that target—or what may be coming at you from the side—then keeping both eyes open is the way to go.

If you only consider your narrowly defined target market when you're developing products, services, or marketing communications, you're doing the equivalent of closing one eye. If you can talk endlessly about what's going on in your industry or sector but have no idea of what's going on in the rest of the world, you're closing one eye. If you provide feedback to an employee without thinking about how that feedback will be interpreted by others on the team, you're closing one eye—and you're missing things.

Over time, I've learned to shoot with both eyes open to the point where it's the most natural thing in the world to me now. That ability is what enabled me to see the woman with the gun, but to also see what else was going on all around her. It ensured that I had all the pertinent information to make the best decision in the moment. It helped me avoid the tunnel vision on the target that could so easily develop in such a situation.

Your ability to figuratively keep both eyes open is the key to avoiding the tunnel vision that can result in suboptimal results. It's not easy. It takes practice. It's something you must train on. But once you get there, you'll never look at things with one eye again.

YOU CAN'T IGNORE THE BYSTANDERS

When it comes to policing, we're acutely aware that we're accountable for every round (bullet) that we fire. On TV, they can just get into a shoot-out and go to lunch afterwards. Not in real life.

In the best-case scenario, there's a boatload of paperwork and questions to be answered both internally and externally. In the worst-case scenario, an errant shot hits an innocent bystander or a fellow officer. My youngest daughter is well trained by now to recognize this. When we're watching a television show, and police are converging on a suspect from all sides with guns drawn, she yells, "Crossfire!" at the screen, knowing that if the police in that scenario were to open fire, they'd likely hit each other.

Say you're chasing a suspect with a gun. They're running down a crowded street, and there are innocent pedestrians, people in shops, and passengers in cars and buses. The suspect turns and shoots at you. Do you return fire? Your answer depends on a lot of things. But one thing's certain—you'd better be able to describe, in detail, what was going on and what led you to the determination that firing your weapon was the most reasonable course of action. That means you must be aware.

The tendency might be to develop tunnel vision. You're chasing a suspect who has a gun and is firing. You must get that suspect. All you can hear and see is that suspect, but the tunnel vision can create a lot of trouble.

You must see and hear and be able to rationally process all that's going on around that suspect. What if he stops? What if he stops in front of a glass store window? If you miss, where is that round going to stop? Who else could it hit? What's the safest thing to do right now for everybody concerned (including the people they might encounter if they get away)?

Now, take away all the other people and all the other concerns. It's just you and a suspect who has a gun and is firing at you. The decision as to whether to return fire just got a whole lot easier, but that's not the world any of us lives in. There are always people and other considerations beyond our target.

At work, you've likely experienced a day of putting out fires. You wake up one Monday morning and you see you already have a text or an email that you know is going to blow up your day, if not your week. Your boss has gotten an urgent request from their boss who has gotten a question from the board of directors that they can't answer. It seems like a simple question. But it's not.

Of course, your boss can't answer it either. You get to the office and it's all hands on deck. Everything else that was already a priority for the day is now pushed to the side. Your team spends the entire day researching, crunching numbers, and putting together a deck. Then your boss rewrites the entire deck and asks you to dig into it deeper.

By the end of the day, your team is exhausted. Frustration is high and job satisfaction is low. Your sales team is angry because you made them miss a deadline with their customer, who is now angry with them.

Finally, the analysis is done. Your boss attempts to present the findings to their boss, but they're not there. They've gone home already, and it turns out this question was not a big deal to them after all. They were just reacting to the board member and passed the buck down the line. In their mind, it was a simple question, and they had no intention of taking up an entire team's day on it.

The problem was that your boss's boss had one eye closed. And everyone right down the line kept one eye closed. And the collateral damage was extensive.

SEEING BEYOND YOUR TARGET:
THE SECONDARY TARGETS AND THE INFLUENCERS

In the previous example, failing to see beyond the target resulted in ripple effects downstream. Many times, in business and marketing, the effects you must be most aware of are the ones that ripple *upstream.*

One area of concern should be secondary targets. This often comes into effect when the purchaser of the product or service you're marketing is not the actual end consumer of that product or service. For instance, mom might be making the purchase on a product you market and sell in grocery stores, but the kids or dad will be the person who actually consumes the product. It's important to not just become laser-focused on your target. You also have to understand how your product and marketing plays with secondary targets and the actual consumers of the product. You must keep both eyes open.

When I worked for the Campbell Soup Company, the media and marketing for most soup products were targeted directly at women. While the women consumed a good deal of the soup sold (especially tomato soup), we also knew that a significant percentage was being served to the rest of the family, specifically the kids.

Grilled cheese and tomato soup is a classic and a tradition in families, dating back for decades. Because it has a warm, healthful, and nostalgic feel to it, we would regularly bring back old advertising that tugged at the heartstrings. And our target—moms—loved it.

And this is where complacency can sneak in. We know our target, and we know what's important to them. We know what pushes their emotional buttons. We know what they want their kids and families to eat and that they need convenience in their meal preparation. We feel comfortable that we understand our target and secondary targets so well that we develop tunnel vision. We close one eye and focus in.

By knowing how our target considers all the people around them, we can convince ourselves that we've considered everyone's point of view. But we're really only considering *our target's* point of view of those things and people around them. And it's not the same thing.

In doing so, we might miss that kids are looking to be more involved in their meal choices and that kids in the same household may have varying tastes and want something specific to themselves. We might also miss that kids have way more options than ever when it comes to convenient meals, and they aren't that interested in nostalgia—it might even make them think of their moms as old-fashioned or boring. And moms *don't* want that.

And so, we find that our advertising, which tests so well with our target, may have a negative effect on the people who influence that target. And now our target is less likely to purchase our product. This is a consequence of our laser focus becoming tunnel vision—of keeping one eye shut.

If we're keeping both eyes open and really observing and becoming aware of what lies beyond the target, we may shift some of our research from mom to the kids. This allows us to learn that, while tomato soup has broad appeal from a taste profile, it can very quickly be seen as tired and old and boring. And this pushes us towards a campaign that repositions tomato soup into a base that can be customized in countless ways by allowing each family member to add their own toppings like sour cream, pepperoni, cheese, Goldfish crackers, etc.

This shift in thought resulted in a successful Campbell's Tomato

Soup Possibilities campaign that reinvigorated the product and allowed us to succeed with our target by seeing beyond it.

Sometimes, though, you must look even further beyond the target to those that you might not typically consider having a stake in or even caring about your product or category.

HOW COULD THEY BE SO TONE-DEAF?

Have you ever seen an advertising campaign and thought to yourself, "How could they be so tone-deaf? How could they get that message so wrong?"

In most situations when you're having that thought, you probably weren't even the intended target for the ad. The product or service may not have been meant for you, but it might have been meant for someone you know, someone you're related to, or someone you talk with and potentially influence. Or, it might have offended you so much that you felt compelled to voice an opinion or get involved. And then, the campaign blows up in the face of the advertiser, not because it angered or upset its target, but because it had an unintended negative impact on what lies beyond the target.

In 2017, Pepsi launched a now infamous advertisement featuring American media personality and social media influencer Kendall Jenner. In the ad, meant to allude to public concerns over racial discrimination and police uses of force, Jenner is in the middle of a fashion shoot when she notices a nearby protest march in the streets. She then joins the march, grabs a Pepsi, and hands it to a police officer—seemingly bridging a gap and bringing a happy conclusion to the strife.

Pepsi's target is primarily people in the 13 to 34 age range, but it often focuses on the younger part of that scale. In particular, Pepsi has heavily used partnerships with celebrities and social media to reach this younger demographic.[32]

Within this target group, Kendall Jenner was hugely popular and seen as a trendsetter. It's likely the ad was seen as light-hearted and was favorably received by the target. However, the ad was seen by a much, much broader group of people. Many were incensed by the seeming implication that Pepsi was minimizing the Black Lives Matter movement and appropriating the rash of protests about police shootings of African Americans happening around the country at the time.

The backlash was swift and harsh. The ad was roasted on mainstream media and social media alike. Pepsi quickly backtracked. According to Pepsi, it was "…trying to project a global message of unity, peace, and understanding. Clearly, we missed the mark, and we apologize. We did not intend to make light of any serious issue. We are removing the content and halting any further rollout."[33]

So, what happened? Likely the spot was tested and performed well with the intended target. However, Pepsi failed to look *beyond* the target to see what the potential reactions and implications might be. They closed an eye and became so laser-focused that they developed tunnel vision. And the results were disastrous.

Sometimes, though, it feels like no research was done at all. That same year, Dove posted on Facebook a video ad regarding cleanliness that showed a black woman taking off her shirt to reveal…a white woman?[34] Using the terminology of this chapter, that might be an example of keeping *both* eyes shut. Not a good strategy.

UNINTENDED CONSEQUENCES AT THE OFFICE

This concept of being aware of your target and beyond applies to most everything. Consider a situation in the office. You're having issues with a specific employee. You decide to discipline them. In your mind, this issue is between them (the target) and you.

But it's not. It's between you and everyone else on the team, maybe even everyone in the office or organization, depending on where you sit. While you may be required to keep your communication with them private, they have no such responsibility, and you can't control their conversations with everyone else. If you understand that idea, then you can take the steps you need to in advance to ensure you're setting the right tone in the office. You can make sure the team dynamics are crafted and that your style and rationale for decision-making are understood. You can set the context for actions and reactions.

In one scenario, you only consider the target, and any perception outside of the target is left to chance. In the other scenario, you curate an office culture and a basic understanding that prescribes that the feelings and perceptions of the people beyond the immediate target are considered and reflected.

This is made even more important by the fact that office culture is one of the places where complacency can really hide in an organization. Problems with the culture can be hidden for long periods of time before the implications are felt. People may suck it up and not complain. A toxic culture can even produce solid short-term results. People at the top levels may be riding high on apparent financial success, blissfully unaware of the troubles bubbling below. Even when they start to see the side effects—increased turnover, difficulty in recruiting new talent, decreased productivity, and workplace hostility or dissatisfaction—they might be more likely to place blame on specific people, teams, or outside dynamics than realizing it is all emanating from their corporate culture.

KEEP BOTH EYES OPEN AND SEE BEYOND THE TARGET TO PREVENT SITUATIONAL COMPLACENCY

As you've learned throughout this chapter, unintended consequences are just unconsidered consequences that have come to fruition. They're a symptom of situational complacency, which can also be called tunnel vision, and they're largely preventable.

Remember, complacency is self-satisfaction accompanied by the unawareness of actual dangers or deficiencies. By solely focusing on your target, you may even succeed in the short term. You may become lulled into thinking it's only your target that matters.

But as we've seen, in police work, business, and at home, there are actual dangers to ignoring what lies beyond the target. Your responsibility is to create a mindset and a culture that understands that, and actively works to keep both eyes open, avoid tunnel vision, and identify and address your target and beyond.

CHAPTER SIX VIGILANCE CHECK

Ask yourself:

1. Where are you keeping one eye closed? What are you potentially missing?

2. Who or what lies beyond your target? Who are the secondary targets? Who are the influencers?

3. What unintended consequences can you anticipate and avoid?

4. Where has your organization been tone-deaf? How could it have been avoided?

CHAPTER SEVEN

___

Reminders: Tap the Senses to Remember What You'd Rather Forget

Between their locker room and the field, the University of Notre Dame football team travels down a flight of steps and through a tunnel. As the players emerge from the stairway into the tunnel, there's a sign, painted in the team's gold and blue colors, that's mounted on the wall above their heads. The sign reads, "PLAY LIKE A CHAMPION TODAY."

It's a simple message, really. You might argue that a scholarship player at a fabled and revered Division I powerhouse shouldn't need the reminder. But to the players, those five simple words mean so much more. Tradition dictates that each player hits that sign as they pass under it. The symbolism is legendary, and the meaning is deep.

The sign was hung there in 1986 by former coach Lou Holtz. According to Holtz, he told the players, "Every time you hit this sign, I want you to remember all the great people that played here before you, all the sacrifices that your teammates have made for you, all the people, your coaches, your parents, who are responsible for you being here."[35]

To this day, the sign still hangs, and the team still hits it when they go underneath. As described in a 2004 article from the Notre Dame website, the sign communicates a great deal to the players, who are reminded that they came to Notre Dame to be champions.[36] It makes them aware that what's at stake is more than just a game—it's about history and tradition. The sign has had so much impact that players can vividly remember the first time they ever touched it.

Perhaps most important in terms of the team's overall success, the sign puts them in the moment and helps guard against any over-confidence, smugness, or self-satisfaction they may have had. It promotes vigilance and defeats complacency.

The sign isn't just a visual reminder. There's a tactile element as well—the hitting of the sign. Of course, there's also an auditory element—the sound of the hand hitting the sign combined with the sounds of the team swarming into the tunnel. The combination of these creates a reminder that brings back everything their coaches have told them and bundles it together into a package that makes their mission clear. It's the last message they receive before entering the field. It's timely, meaningful, and impactful. And they carry that memory with them for a lifetime.

WOULD YOU LIKE TO START WITH SOME JUICE OR COFFEE?

I used to work for the Minute Maid division within the Coca-Cola Company. My role was a hybrid sales/marketing position. Basically, I worked with sales teams servicing what we called our "Immediate

Consumption" customers (i.e., venues where our products were consumed in the venue as opposed to bought and consumed elsewhere). These included restaurants, hotels, theme parks, airlines, etc.

Our goal was to become the trusted partner of our customer. We did that by showing a dedication to growing their bottom line, which, of course, also included selling more of our products.

One key strategy for this in the restaurant business is the upsell. If you've ever been asked if you wanted fries with that, you've been upsold. It's a simple and powerful tool to increase the average check. Success hinges on the ability to get the server (or cashier) to do the upsell.

This, of course, applies more broadly than just to the restaurant business. In 2014, for example, JetBlue expected to earn $190 million from simply upselling passengers on more space. In the broader travel industry, 48 percent of airline passengers and 59 percent of people staying in hotels report that they have interest in available upgrades in products and services.[37]

As a result, a lot of time is spent educating and training employees. Even in situations where it seems to be in the best interest of the employee to upsell—such as those working for tips where the increase in average check will directly result in increased earnings—it's hard to get 100 percent participation.

The reality is that people forget. They get busy with all the other things they have going on. Combine that with the fact that they may not be totally comfortable asking for the extra sales (or feeling like a salesperson), and the upsell often gets overlooked. So, we'd look for ways to provide reminders, such as back-of-house flyers, point-of-sale terminal prompts, and table tents. All were tactics meant to do one thing—remind the employees to upsell.

WHY WE FORGET

"Your mind is for having ideas, not holding them."—David Allen[38]

The mind is built to focus on the present. As such, our brain is designed to forget much of what we experience. It must for practical purposes. How could we move forward if previous experiences consumed our thought processes in the present?

According to McGill University researcher Oliver Hardt, "without forgetting, we would have no memory at all." Hardt further asserts that remembering everything would be inefficient, because our brains would be overrun with useless memories. "Forgetting serves as a filter."[39]

Most of what we see, do, and experience throughout a day does not serve a purpose as a memory. We don't need to remember what the person sitting next to us on an airplane was wearing or all the numbers on all the spreadsheets we've prepared and presented, for example.

We obviously, though, remember at least some things. And, for evolutionary purposes, humans are hardwired to remember bad memories more than good ones. It's a hand-me-down trait from cavemen, who lived or died based on their ability to be alert to bad things. This trait stays with us today, and it helps to keep us safe.

According to Rick Hanson, PhD, founder of the Wellspring Institute for Neuroscience and Contemplative Wisdom, our brain's amygdala "uses about two-thirds of its neurons to look for bad news. Once it sounds the alarm, negative events and experiences get quickly stored in memory, in contrast to positive events and experiences, which usually need to be held in awareness for a dozen or more seconds to transfer from short-term memory buffers to long-term storage."[40]

So, the brain is designed to forget. But it's also programmed to re-member negative events more than positive ones. Why, then, do we still forget the things that have happened in the past that *should* make us the most vigilant? Why aren't we constantly conscious of bad things that have happened so that we can better avoid them in the future? How can cops (and soldiers, health-care professionals, etc.) see so many awful things and still function?

The answer is self-preservation. The mind, in its mission to allow us to succeed, is normally very good at helping us become desensitized to things that previously made us scared or stressed. Each time we're exposed to the stimuli that has been associated with fear or trauma and we don't experience a negative result, we can become desensi-tized to it to the point where that negative association no longer affects us.

According to Dr. Bruce Harry, an associate professor of clinical psy-chiatry and forensic psychiatry at the University of Missouri School of Medicine, "our central nervous system basically shuts down past a point." Essentially, the brain protects us by providing emotional distance from the traumatic events. "It's the brain's way of trying to keep you healthy."[41] You can see why this is important. An inability to do so could logically lead to debilitating PTSD.

In our Sheriff's department, we had multiple incidents over a couple of years where calls that involved people with mental illness resulted in devastating outcomes. In one, a man who was reported as being suicidal ended up getting into a gun battle while driving towards a school and hospital, ultimately shooting and paralyzing Detective Dan Brite before being killed while he was fleeing.[42] In another, pre-viously mentioned in Chapter One, a series of calls about a disturbance turned into situation where a barricaded person with mental illness ambushed and shot several deputies, killing Deputy Zackari Parrish before killing himself.[43]

As you might imagine, in the immediate aftermath of calls like these, you get an increased tingle in the back of your neck when similar calls come up. You remember everything that happened those days. You remember what happened to your colleagues (and their families). You consider all the things that could go wrong. You wait for backup. You approach things slowly.

Over time, though, as you go on more and more of those calls and have favorable outcomes, your mind relaxes. You let go of the vividly bad memories, the fears, and the anxieties. You have to if you're going to keep doing the job.

Some of this can be explained by the idiom about getting back on the horse. As the mind learns that the action that once caused you harm (physically or emotionally) won't necessarily do so in the future, you learn to suppress the bad memory. You don't forget that the events happened. If someone starts talking about falling off a horse, you'll no doubt remember your fall very vividly. But you're able to push away the fear and the anxiety a little more with each successful ride.

You may even find that, right after the fall, you wear safety gear religiously. But, as you get further away from that incident in your mind, and as you become desensitized, you may begin to ease your use of safety gear, convincing yourself you no longer need it or it's too burdensome or restrictive and the risks don't warrant it.

And this, of course, is when complacency settles in.

PREGNANCY AMNESIA?

I sometimes joke that my wife and I suffered from pregnancy amnesia.

Our first pregnancy wasn't what you'd call a joy. Sometimes I hear others talk about how great pregnancy was: The pregnant woman felt great. She glowed. The couple stayed in shape together. It was wonderful.

I usually smile and nod when they relate those stories to me. All the while, I am fantasizing about poking them right in the middle of their forehead and telling them about our experience (which, I am sure, was still better than many).

My wife was sick the entire time. She couldn't leave the house without something to use as a barf bag. She didn't feel like she was glowing. She was happy to be pregnant and looking forward to having a child. But it was sometimes hard to tell if she was looking forward to having a child or just looking forward to having a child *outside of her*.

You get the point. It wasn't pleasant. And after our daughter was born, things didn't get much easier. We had a hard time getting her to nurse, and she didn't sleep.

Suffice it to say that, during this time, we weren't super excited about trying for child number two. And then, miraculously, a couple of years later, we forgot how bad it had been. We somehow remembered the experience as way more positive than it was. And our love for our daughter was immense. And, after the first year, things got *much* easier. And after two years, we decided to have another. And I'm glad we did. That pregnancy was easier, but it was experienced while having to care for a toddler. And, if I'm being honest, it still wasn't fun. So, we stopped at two.

Perhaps you've experienced something like this at work. You find the organization repeating painful processes every few years, just long enough for a lot of the people who were involved the last time to either be gone or to be in different positions where they won't feel the pain. It could be a reorganization, downsizing, budget cuts, vendor reviews, or something else. When you are going through it, you think, "Never again." But then it happens again. People and organizations develop amnesia.

AMNESIA THROUGH ATTRIBUTIONAL BIAS

Sometimes, we're able to forget the lessons from painful failures or bad experiences because we can convince ourselves that the blame really lies somewhere other than on us.

In a *Harvard Business Review* article titled, "Why Serial Entrepreneurs Don't Learn From Failure," the authors define serial entrepreneurs as ones who start multiple businesses but do them one at a time in succession.[44]

In a survey of 576 UK-based entrepreneurs, the authors found that these serial entrepreneurs were significantly more likely than others to remain overoptimistic about their ability to succeed in their new ventures, even after suffering previous failures. In hypothesizing why this was the case, the authors wrote the following:

Paradoxically, serial entrepreneurs' greater propensity to remain overoptimistic may be due in part to the deep pain, even trauma, they feel when their projects fail—pain that is especially acute precisely

because they involve themselves in only one business at a time.
Psychological research suggests that strong emotions often prompt
people to blame others or external events rather than themselves
so that they can maintain some semblance of self-esteem and a
sense of control. This "attributional bias" appears to make serial
entrepreneurs less capable of learning from failure than portfolio
entrepreneurs, whose attachment is spread among multiple initiatives.

Have you ever experienced a situation at work when a coworker is so emotionally and personally invested in a project that they're able to rationalize away its failure on external people or events? Does this make it more or less likely that the lessons that could be gleaned from that failure are realized, preserved, and used to avoid future pain?

THE NEED TO REMEMBER

As we've discussed, a certain amount of amnesia is necessary to mentally survive as a law enforcement officer. We experience deaths—both of strangers and people who are close to us. We see the pitfalls and severe negative consequences that could result from certain behaviors or attitudes. To make it, you must have a unique ability to compartmentalize. You must be able to feel and deal with things, while also putting those feelings in a neat little box and filing them away so they don't interfere with your day-to-day activities. We must allow ourselves to forget, to desensitize.

At the same time, we must ensure we don't forget about the people and the events and their lessons in the moment. We must remember all the things we told ourselves we would do differently. All the plans we made during our grieving. These are the things that quickly fade once we're back on the job, because that's what our brains need to do to keep us focused.

It's no different in business. A certain amount of amnesia is just as necessary to survive as a boss or an employee—or a parent or, really, just as a human being. If you carried all your experiences with you all the time, you'd find it very hard to function at all. And if you've ever brought your frustrations from the office home with you, or brought your home issues to work, you know that things can get muddy quickly.

At work, hard times always come. Budgets get cut. Efficiencies are found. Belts are tightened. Boots are strapped.

Then things get better, and the organization breathes a sigh of relief and gets back to normal—meaning a little more wasteful, a little lazier, and a bit more relaxed. You don't necessarily forget the big global recession or the pandemic. But you forget the lessons, because you get back to normal and your normal self doesn't want to think about that stuff.

But just like in law enforcement, it's important to remember the lessons from these times you'd rather forget—the things you learned that you must do differently in the future.

MEMENTO

The movie *Memento*, made in 2000 and starring Guy Pearce, is still one of my favorites.[45] In it, Pearce plays a character who suffers from short-term memory loss, which prevents him from remembering what happens to him throughout the film. In fact, his short-term memory seems to reset about every 15 minutes.

Throughout the movie, Pearce's character is trying to solve a murder mystery of great importance to him. To keep himself moving towards the answer, he utilizes a maze of Polaroids and tattoos to remind him of important information he knows he will quickly forget. The movie alternates between a forward-moving and a backward-moving timeline. It's super unique and cool, but that's not the point.

The point is Pearce's character uses these reminders to keep him vigilant and moving towards his ultimate goal. Of course, he suffers from frustrating and debilitating memory loss (which he's acutely aware of) that I hope none of us ever has to experience. But the reality is that we all, as humans, suffer from memory loss every day. We must. Our brains just can't and won't hold onto everything.

While that memory loss can keep us sane and productive, it can also lead to complacency by allowing us to put aside the memories of dangers and pitfalls from our past experiences that would help us guard ourselves from repeating past mistakes (of our own doing, or someone else's).

While tattoos and Polaroids may not be the answer for most of us, the lesson about the value of effectively using reminders is valid, nonetheless.

THE ELEPHANT STATUETTE

We know that our brain is designed to forget. And it protects us by trying to forget traumatic memories. So how can we make sure we hold on to the lessons from those memories to guard against complacency in the future? The answer may lie in associating sensory cues with those memories to bring them to the forefront in the exact times we need them the most.

In 2016, Harvard Professor Todd Rogers and University of Pennsylvania Professor Katherine Milkman published a research article in *Psychological Science* titled, "Reminders Through Association."[46] In it, they detailed their study that showed how associating intentions with specific cues significantly increases your ability to act on those intentions.

In one study, they took two groups of people and told them that when they exited the study, they could have $1 donated to a charity simply by quietly taking a paper clip from a pile on the way out of the office. The $1 would not come from their fee; it was completely incremental. Surprisingly, only 89 percent of the people said they intended to take the paper clip to trigger the $1 donation. I don't want to even consider what the other 11 percent were thinking!

Regardless, only those 89 percent were kept in the study, so everyone remaining had the intention of triggering the $1 donation. Half the group was given the following reminder before they were released: "Thank you! To remind you to pick up a paper clip, an elephant statuette will be sitting on the counter as you collect your payment." In their message was a picture of an elephant statuette. The people in the other group were given the simple message of "Thank you," but were not told about the elephant statuette. The researchers then recorded which participants took a paper clip on the way out.

Seventy-four percent of the people who were told about the elephant statuette and shown the picture of what the elephant would look like remembered to take the paper clip. Only 42 percent of those in the control group took the paper clip. Keep in mind that every one of those people indicated they had an intention to take the paper clip.

Further into the study, the authors determined that while both the written reminder and an image to associate with the reminder drove significant improvements over those without either, the visual cue was significantly more powerful in its effects, especially when distinctive related to other things surrounding it.

In this part of the study, the researchers showed how an organization can use "reminders through association" to help their clients do what they intended. They went to a coffee shop and, as people exited the store, gave out coupons that would be valid two days later. Everyone was given a flyer to remind them to use the coupon when they see the cash register. The test group's flyer also included a picture of a green toy alien and the message that the alien would be on the register to help remind them. The control group, however, was not told about the toy alien.

As a result, 24 percent of the customers who were told about the toy alien remembered to use the coupons. Only 17 percent of those who were not told about the toy alien remembered to use the coupon. That's a 41 percent increase in effectiveness through the association of the image of the toy alien.

In the journal article, "Words Versus Pictures: Leveraging the Research on Visual Communications," Pauline Dewan asserts that "… pictures are not only more effortless to recognize and process than words, but also easier to recall. When words enter long-term memory, they do so with a single code. Pictures on the other hand, contain two codes: one visual and the other verbal, each stored in different places in the brain. The dual-coding nature of images allows for two independent ways of accessing visual memories, increasing the odds of remembering at least one of them."[47]

So, it's logical to conclude that cues are vital in remembering intentions, and further, cues that tap into more areas of the brain increase their effectiveness.

WHAT ARE THOSE WRISTBANDS?

One of my favorite things to do as a police officer is to interact with children. Their purity, joy, curiosity, and sense of wonder are always a boost to the soul. Sometimes, I get to work special assignments that involve going from elementary school to elementary school—for community peace of mind, but also to just mingle with the kids in classrooms, the hallways, and the playground. We have fun. We play kickball. I read to them. They ask to be Tased or handcuffed. (No lie—follow an officer in uniform into a crowded elementary school lunchroom and count the number of kids who ask if they can get either Tased or handcuffed. Or both!)

They also have questions about all the items on my duty belt. They want to know about my gun, my Taser, my handcuffs, and my baton, and why I carry so many flashlights ("One is none, two is one," I always reply). Their curiosity provides lots of opportunities. I'm able to build a relationship with them, so they feel comfortable with police instead of scared. I always get a laugh out of the younger ones when I tell them I'm going to show them my cop glasses and hold a pair of handcuffs up to my eyes.

Inevitably, they also ask me about the two wristbands I have on my handcuff case. I never mind telling them, even though the wristbands serve as reminders to me of the two incidents involving Deputies Parrish and Brite that I described earlier in this chapter.

The wristbands don't just represent tragedy. They also represent bravery, heroism, honor, respect, and many other situation-specific lessons that are personal to me. They are made of black silicone and have embossed white lettering on them. Half of each includes the name of the person being honored and their badge number. The other half reads, "NO ONE FIGHTS ALONE." Two blue lines fill the space on either side.

The reality is that those wristbands are my reminders through association. I place them on my cuff case for a specific reason. Numerous times during a shift, I rest my right hand on that cuff case. My hand is usually there when I'm talking with a suspect. When my hand touches the top of the case, I feel the two wristbands, the stretchiness of the silicone, and the texture of the words imprinted on them. When I feel them, my mind instinctively thinks of Parrish and Brite and what I'm supposed to remember—to be vigilant.

It's all subconscious, of course, but the reminders are real. When I feel those wristbands, my senses heighten. I check my stance and my position relative to the person I'm talking with. I scan my surroundings. I'm more aware.

TAPPING THE SENSES TO REMEMBER

We all know there are five senses: smell, taste, touch, sight, and sound. We now know that an effective way of reminding ourselves to stay vigilant is by creating cues that tap more than one of those senses and deliver messages in a timely manner at the time they are most relevant.

There are several ways we accomplish this in law enforcement. We obviously use a lot of visual cues—the words on our patrol cars, the pins we wear on our uniforms, and the signage in our briefing rooms and parking lots. These cues are effective in evoking memories in the moment, but their effects are fleeting and not necessarily linked closely in time or proximity to the situations we will most need them in. Plus, we already know that the more we can connect these visual cues to other senses, the more powerful they will be.

Earlier in the book I mentioned the Below 100 posters that are in our briefing rooms and on the gates as we leave the parking lot. These are the posters that are provided to us by the Below 100 organization, whose mission is to reduce line-of-duty deaths to fewer than 100 per year. They aim to achieve this mission by eliminating "preventable line-of-duty police deaths and serious injuries through compelling common-sense training designed to focus on areas under an officer's control."[48]

The posters remind us to do the following:

- Wear our vests.

- Wear our safety belts.

- Watch our speed.

- WIN (What's Important Now).

- Remember: Complacency Kills.

We see them every day, and I'd be lying if I said there aren't times when catching sight of the sign triggers me to fasten my seatbelt as I exit the parking lot.

A visual reminder is great in the moment. I see it and it reminds me about something that I might not otherwise consider. But what happens once I'm out of the lot and on patrol? That's where the sense of sound comes in. It's simple really. If I get in my patrol car and start moving without fastening my belt, that annoying beeping sound starts. The sound then immediately triggers the image of the Below 100 sign in my head and makes me think how dumb I would feel if someone had to explain to my family that I wasn't coming home because I didn't buckle up. And the seatbelt goes on.

It's the same way the feel of my wristbands immediately reminds me of the messages imprinted on each and brings me into sharper focus on officer safety in the moment.

HOW TO MAKE REMINDERS WORK FOR YOU

Here are some guidelines for how you can best use reminders in your business life to fight complacency and encourage the most desired behaviors:

- **Leverage a sense.** Find the best sense to tap into. Try to use the sense that's most closely related to what you're trying to remember. All the senses are tied to memory, but if you can find a way to leverage smell or taste, they're the strongest. You've probably done this at home by frying up some bacon when you want the family to wake up and come for breakfast! Some businesses do a great job of leveraging the sense of smell in their environment. Think about the smell of popcorn in a movie theatre or the smell of coconuts in the swimsuit department of a clothing store. For a lot of businesses, taste or smell might be tough senses to tap into, but sound is a lot more accessible. In a warehouse, the beeping sound of a forklift coming is meant to break through the noise and make everyone think of safety as they are moving around. Don't shy away from simple visual reminders, though, if that's all you have to work with. In the office, you might use a sign or even sticky notes to serve as reminders.

- **Make it distinct**. What happens when you have too many signs, too many yellow sticky notes, or too much beeping in the warehouse? The less distinctive the cues are, the less effective they are, and the more they fade into the background. What's your "PLAY LIKE A CHAMPION TODAY" sign? Your elephant statuette? Your green alien toy? The thing that's going to get noticed and remembered because it stands out and it's different?

- **Be selective**. Focus on the things that are most important at the time. Keep the number of reminders to the bare minimum and the most critical. In the movie *Office Space*, Jennifer Aniston's character works at a fast casual restaurant (fashioned after TGI Fridays). She was harassed by her boss for not having enough flair (buttons and pins) on her uniform's suspenders. It was a joke, but based in reality. Too much flair—too many cues—end up reminding us of nothing in particular. They become background and lose their effectiveness. Fun aside: Not long after the movie, TGI Fridays did away with their own flair. *Office Space* creator Mike Judge was convinced that we (and every TGI Fridays server) have him to thank![49]

- **Now, leverage more than one sense at a time**. Try to incorporate more than one sense into your reminder. The more senses you can tap into, the stickier the message will be. And they don't have to be through the same reminder. Think text reminder combined with elephant statuette, the Below 100 sign combined with the car beeping when the seatbelt isn't done, flashing lights combined with beeping to alert to safety concerns in a warehouse, or the toy alien in the coffee shop. In a retail environment, it could be a message combined with a tone at checkout to remind about the upsell opportunities. In a classroom, a teacher may clap three times to cue attention (the visual of the clapping combined with the sound is more effective than just the teacher asking for silence).

- **Think internally and externally**. Reminders that tap into internal *and* external interests can generate powerful results. Think of the wristband example. Not only do they mean something to me (internal), but they also provide an opportunity for others to become curious and ask about them (external). This is also the idea behind No-Shave-November and other such campaigns that involve growing a mustache or beard. Not only is the participant reminded each day as they see themselves in the mirror or stroke their facial hair with their hands, but they also provide an opportunity to talk to others about their messages when they get asked why they haven't shaved. Wearable messages can be very effective. An interesting T-shirt or hat or pin or sticker. Something that represents a core internal imperative—but also generates external curiosity. These messages should be subtle and not scream for attention. But they're a great way to educate the outside world while also giving your employees opportunities to further internalize the messages by repeating them and using them to educate. Another great example from military and law enforcement is the Challenge Coin. A Challenge Coin is something that may be carried by people working together in a unit or a division or even an organization that identifies them to each other and helps to improve morale. The coins themselves have a message or a meaning to those who carry them. The message is reinforced every time they feel them in a pocket. And when others see such a coin, they'll inevitably ask about it, which gives the owner an opportunity to explain what it is and what it communicates.

- **You don't have to spend a lot of money**. You can spend less than $2.50 each if you order as few as five custom wristbands. If you order thousands, they are less than 15 cents each. I'm not saying you should be doing wristbands. As mentioned above, pins, T-shirts, hats, stickers, or Challenge Coins all can have assigned meaning. Really anything could do the job. The message is that you don't have to spend a lot of money; you just have to find the right message and the right way to deliver it. Best-selling author (*Fanocracy*) and past Brand ManageCamp conference speaker David Meerman Scott is a *big* fan of stickers. In his book, he details how the stickers on his laptop (especially the one of the Grateful Dead) allowed him to quickly bond and form a relationship with Brian Halligan, the co-founder and CEO of HubSpot, during a meeting they had in 2007. Their shared experiences that were represented by the stickers allowed them to gain an immediate and deep understanding of each other that a mere conversation would never have been able to accomplish. They went on to work together, write together (*Marketing Lessons from the Grateful Dead*), and go to over 50 Grateful Dead shows together.[50] The power of reminders is not tied to a price tag.

- **Don't make yourself crazy over the creative**. And you don't have to be super overt with the message. Find the word or words or image or taste or smell or sound that best communicates the message and go with it. Just feeling the embossed letters on my wristbands reminds me of many messages and lessons. It's not the words or letters themselves; it's what they represent. It might just be your logo. Or your tagline. Or an acronym for a major internal initiative. Or a toy alien. It's not so much the actual execution but more about how that specific execution is distinct and connects with what it is you are trying to remind yourself or others to do.

- **Don't overdo it**. Stay focused on the most important reminders. Don't over-flair!

Remember, our brains would rather allow us to forget the particulars of painful memories, of times things went wrong. The danger is that as we forget those things, we also forget the warning signs and the lessons.

Follow the simple guidelines above to develop the reminders you need to stay vigilant and avoid complacency. They'll serve to interrupt and awaken the mind in the times where you are most likely to be lulled, overconfident, or unaware. And, as a bonus, when tied to business imperatives, they may even help you drive revenue.

CHAPTER SEVEN VIGILANCE CHECK

Ask yourself:

1. What do you or your business need to remember, but would rather forget?

2. What things could you, your team, or your organization benefit from by making sure they remain top of mind?

3. What are some visual cues you could utilize to keep important messages front and center? As a thought starter, consider office space/environment (e.g., "PLAY LIKE A CHAMPION" sign; the elephant statuette; things that sit on a desk, wall, door, or floor; a piece of machinery; etc.), personal space (wristbands or clothing), and possessions that travel (phone cases, laptop stickers or skins, bags or luggage, pens, books, etc.).

4. How can you bring multiple senses together to make a stronger reminder? How can you layer in sound, touch, smell, or taste on top of a visual reminder?

CHAPTER EIGHT

———

Autonomy: Fighting Complacency through the Power of Empowerment

Consider this situation, which happens all the time: We get a call from the loss-prevention officer at a local big-name general merchandise or food retailer. They have an 18-year-old suspect detained in their office. The suspect was caught attempting to shoplift about $100 of goods from the store. They have video. The young suspect is being cooperative. There was no struggle and no violence. The loss-prevention officer doesn't believe the suspect has any weapons. The store would like to press charges.

As I head to the call, I'm already playing through what I know and what options I have. Assuming the story as relayed is 100 percent correct, I've got a nonviolent adult who committed theft without using or displaying any weapons. The $100 would represent a third-degree misdemeanor, which is the lowest level of misdemeanor in Colorado.

I run the suspect through my computer and find that they don't have any warrants, and there's no criminal history that I can see.

Knowing what I know, before I even arrive, I'm aware that I have some discretion in this situation. With the store wanting to pursue charges, just letting it go with a stern warning is not in the cards. Because it's a misdemeanor, though, I have the option of taking the suspect to jail or releasing them on a summons with a court date sometime in the future.

Because I have choices, I'm already thinking about what I need to determine to make that choice. First, I must make sure the suspect is actually unarmed and doesn't have any other contraband or drugs on them (it's nice that the loss-prevention agent said they didn't, but I need to determine that for myself). I'll be looking for their attitude: Is the suspect brazen and rude, or scared and remorseful? Have they had previous run-ins at the store that went undocumented? Why did they commit the crime? Do they have a stable living situation within our jurisdiction or are they transient? Do they have a substance abuse problem? How likely are they to show up for their court date?

I'm also keeping an eye (or ear, really, as I listen on the radio while handling the call) on how busy the rest of the deputies on duty are. Are we short-staffed? Are several people tied up on a complicated call? How hard will it be on everyone else if I must spend two hours out of service while I transport and book them into jail?

My inclination is to cut them loose on a summons unless some reason makes that an untenable solution. If I can find out more about them, I'm also more likely to be able to offer them some help or assistance that could help them avoid making the decision to steal in the future, or offer resources for addiction or help getting to a shelter or getting a hotel room. Maybe I determine the suspect's a good person with a good future who just made a stupid decision based on a dare. Maybe they were forced to do it by an abusive parent.

But the real point here is that I have the autonomy and discretion to make this choice. I don't necessarily need to ask for permission (depending on the circumstances, I may call my sergeant to make sure we're on the same page). There's no one way to go about making the decision. It's up to me to gather the information I need and to make the best choice I can, given the totality of the circumstances and the goal of best serving the greater good for all the involved parties.

Because of that, I'm forced to be engaged. I'm forced to think. I'm forced to be present and aware of all that's going on around me. By default, I'm doing many of the things required to fight complacency.

Now, let's flip that around. Let's assume there was no discretion involved. The suspect got caught stealing, so they go to jail. Many of the things I had to think about earlier are now irrelevant—their attitude, their living arrangements, their family situation, their relationship with drugs. What the staffing levels are in my area could also be largely irrelevant. If I don't have a choice as to whether to take the suspect to jail, it really doesn't matter how short staffed we are anymore, does it?

Less autonomy means more autopilot. In the world of complacency, autopilot is bad. It inhibits thinking. It inhibits questions. It inhibits engagement. And, in turn, it inhibits personal satisfaction, which leads to less engagement, and so on, and so forth.

ENGAGEMENT AT WORK

It's easy to talk about complacency at the corporate and strategic level. There is never a shortage of examples at the macro-level of how an organization, industry, or even a country has become complacent and vulnerable.

Blockbuster did this while Netflix did that. Kodak missed this. Sears didn't do that, and so on. You get it. It's easy to put the focus of the story on the broad organization.

However, it's important to remember that, even if the higher levels of an organization are taking steps to remain vigilant, a great deal of the onus of avoiding complacency will still fall on the front-line employees, those who are doing the blocking and tackling every day. Whether it's the clerk in a retail environment, the fast-food worker, or the factory or warehouse employee, if they become complacent—unaware to the actual dangers and threats around them—the organization is bound to suffer.

Just like in police work, the best way to ensure someone remains vigilant in their day-to-day activities, so they're actively thinking about the role they play and how they can play it better for the organization as a whole, is to keep them *engaged*.

The more engaged someone is in the task they're performing, the higher their level of passion about their work and the more commitment they'll display to their organization and their work effort.

Of course, there are lots of things that can factor into someone's engagement with their job: their career advancement opportunities, their pay, how much they think the organization actually cares about them, and how well the organization communicates.

These are all important, no doubt. And they can play a major role in job satisfaction over time. But their main effect is going to be on overall motivation—not in how engaged someone is *in the moment*. While they can set an overall attitude, they don't have as much ability to dictate the level at which someone's brain is actually involved in thinking, problem solving, and strategizing at a specific point in time.

Let's put it this way. Even if you have all those things—fair pay, career advancement opportunities, good communication, etc.—you're still prone to mentally checking out in the moment because of the way your job allows (or even *encourages*) your brain to do so. So, you can be well paid and still dis-engaged. Alternatively, you can also be poorly paid and super engaged, if the way your job is designed gives you the tools and the freedom to make decisions that can improve outcomes.

So, what's the one element that you can control that can actually promote engagement on the job? What element ensures the brain is working and being leveraged to think through solutions and potential outcomes, and allows the front line to be vigilant?

AUTONOMY

Autonomy is having the freedom to decide (or at least be flexible in) *how* the work should be done. Studies have shown that as autonomy increases, engagement at work and commitment to the job can increase by at least 17 percent. And, not surprisingly, things like job satisfaction and role clarity significantly rise as well.[51]

The more scripted someone's job is, the less flexibility they have in determining how they complete their tasks (or even what the tasks are), and the more likely they are to check out. And once they're checked out, how can they be vigilant? How can they see the unseen threats? How can they be the front line in protecting your organization from complacency?

As we've already seen, autonomy is a major tool that we use in law enforcement. It's a core tenant of how the police officer's job is built. From the first day you work the street, you're given a very, very powerful tool in your tool belt by your department: discretion.

Don't get me wrong. We have a lot of rules, regulations, and, obviously, laws we must follow. And sometimes, we really don't have a choice as to how we do our job. But, in many situations, and especially related to how we handle our calls and the people we interact with, we do.

When we pull over a car for a traffic violation, we most often have several choices. We can write a ticket for the full violation. We can write a ticket for some lesser variation of a violation—for example, pulling someone over who was speeding 17 miles over the speed limit, but writing the ticket for only nine miles over the speed limit, thereby saving the driver money and points on their license. Or we can just let them go with a warning.

As we've discussed, we even have discretion as to how we approach the car. We can walk up to the driver side or to the passenger side. We can call the driver back to us. We *have choices*, which forces us to *make choices*.

There are certainly things that are out of our control. Those who commit domestic violence are going to jail every time. If you have a felony warrant, you're probably going to jail.

Just the fact that some things are within discretion while others are not, forces us to think. It engages our brains. It keeps us in the present. And the byproduct is that it keeps us engaged. And, in our world, that means it keeps us safer.

Sometimes we talk about the things we do in terms of "shall" and "may." Whether it is written in statutes or our department policies, "shall" means we don't have a choice, and "may" means we do. We certainly have both. But most of the time, it's the "mays" that determine how good an officer is.

PIZZA FROM A SHOE STORE?

We all have stories we can tell about bad customer service or call center experiences we've had. For example, you go through a long, winding list of phone-tree options before you finally get an agent on the phone. And then they aren't even able to help you; their hands are tied. You ask to speak to a supervisor. You're placed on hold, ever fearful that they'll lose the call and you'll have to start all over. You finally reach the supervisor, who basically reads you the same script you've already heard. You hang up in frustration, desperate to salvage some feeling of control from this infuriating situation. Unfortunately, this is more often the rule than the exception.

For many companies, the last thing they want you to do is call them. Try to find a phone number on some company's websites—unless, of course, that company is Zappos.

In 2010, I brought in a speaker from Zappos to my Brand Manage-Camp conference. His name is Aaron Magness, and at the time, he was the Senior Director of Brand Marketing and Business Development. Our conference was in Las Vegas, Nevada, as was Zappos's headquarters, so I stopped in for a tour one day when I was in town taking care of some details. A tour. Of an Internet shoe retailer.

It was incredible. I had heard and read about Zappos's fanatical dedication to customer service. But being in the building, I could see it firsthand. Every person I met was happy and peppy and friend-ly. Every workspace was personalized to the individual's personality. Zappos encouraged them to go wild.

I was shown the Zappos culture book, which is used to commu-nicate to anyone interested (new hires, vendors, partners, visitors) what the company is really all about. It's put together by the employ-ees themselves.

I learned that every new Zappos employee, no matter what their job, spends their first four weeks onboarding: learning about the history and core values, working in the call center and taking calls, building relationships, and making sure they enjoy their role. They're not al-lowed to start their real job until they graduate from the onboarding. And then, the graduates are offered cash money *to quit*. They're so serious about not wanting people at Zappos who don't enjoy work-ing there, that they want to take all the barriers out of their decision process. As of 2020, a new employee would get offered one month's salary if they wanted to quit at the end of their orientation.

So, it didn't surprise me when Aaron told a story about a pizza de-livery that has since become the stuff of urban legend. Evidently, the Zappos CEO at the time, the late Tony Hsieh, was with a group of people at a shoe sales conference in Santa Monica. It was late and they'd been out drinking, and when they got back to the hotel, room service was closed. They then found it difficult to find a local restaurant that was open and would deliver food to the hotel. It was then that Hsieh suggested another member of the group (who did not work at Zappos) call the Zappos.com phone number and ask for help. The representative who answered was confused, but unde-terred. She put the group on hold, coming back a couple of minutes later with phone numbers for the closest places to them that were still open and delivering pizzas.

The representative had no idea who was on the phone. She was fairly certain, I'm sure, that no shoes were about to be ordered. She didn't ask for contact info or try to upsell (or sell at all). She did what she had been empowered to do by her training, by her company's commitment to customer service, and by the culture of the work environment. She took care of the customer.

She didn't ask for permission. She didn't read off a script (Zappos doesn't use them). She didn't go through a checklist of topics and promotions. She just took care of the customer. And Tony Hsieh, the CEO, was delighted and proud and fed. This is the difference that autonomy and discretion can have on engagement, satisfaction, and performance.

Contrast this with the situation of a bad customer service call. Can that representative go off script? Are they tasked with making the customer happy, no matter what? Would they research where you could get a pizza? Probably not.

Which representative is more likely to be engaged and satisfied? Which representative is more likely to generate positive outcomes? Which representative is more likely to pick up on cues as to how a disgruntled customer could be saved? Which representative is most likely to report issues, concerns, or findings up the chain with the goal of finding solutions?

If there was a systemic issue, or even the beginning of a trend of concerns, which representative would be most valuable in ensuring it was run up the flagpole as opposed to hidden from view? And what's the result of hiding concerns from the front line from management? They develop overconfidence and complacency, because they don't know better.

MACRO-LEVEL VERSUS MICRO-LEVEL COMPLACENCY

Complacency isn't a concept that applies equally and evenly across all layers of a business, a government, or even a family. It's very possible (even probable) that different layers of people can experience different levels of complacency, all at the same time. The context of their complacency may also be very different.

At the macro-level, senior executives may be vigilantly strategizing about the competition. They're considering brand positioning, targets, pricing, products, store environments, etc.

But at the micro-level, there are the front-line workers who are responsible for executing strategies and being the primary point of contact for the customer. Depending on how their jobs are structured, they may have very different approaches towards their positions. It's entirely possible that they aren't even aware of the potential competitive dangers that exist. It is also entirely possible that they don't care.

The micro-level complacency is no less dangerous than any other. In fact, it's the micro-level complacency—driven by a lack of engagement—that can roll up into the macro-level kind. And that's what makes it so dangerous.

Lack of engagement and motivation at the micro-level—on the front lines of where the organization interacts most directly with the customers or consumers—can lead to a lack of awareness of dangers and a feeling of overconfidence at the macro-levels.

When the regional sales manager already knows exactly what they want the team to execute and they make the team feel as if their input is not valuable, the salespeople with feet on the ground may never feel the opportunity to relay what they're seeing firsthand. Maybe they hear rumblings from customers about new competition or changes in purchasing policies coming down the road. If the front-line employees are purely task executors, that information may never make its way to management. The result? The executives are unaware of the potential threats and are overconfident about their strategies and plans. They are, in effect, complacent—even if they *feel* they're being vigilant.

STIFLED BY MICROMANAGEMENT

Many times, jobs are actually designed to take all the creativity and choices out of the equation. If you work in a factory, you may be tasked with performing the same functions repeatedly. The goal in the repetition is expertise and quality. The cost is autonomy and engagement. That's why it's so important in those situations to have external reminders about safety. It's just too easy to get lulled into the repetition, become overconfident, lose track of the dangers around you, and ultimately, get hurt or cause someone else to get hurt.

This type of prescribed work activity isn't usually the case in an office job. Sure, there are tasks to do, but you don't often have a specific checklist that spells out exactly how you must do each one.

In the office, we have a different problem altogether: the micromanaging boss. You know the ones. They hover. They meddle. They always want you doing things their way.

In a study performed by Accountemps, a leading staffing company, 59 percent of employees who were interviewed reported they had worked for a micromanaging boss at some point in their careers. Of those, 68 percent said it negatively impacted their morale, and 55 percent said it decreased their productivity.[52]

Think about how you feel when you're being micromanaged. When you know it isn't going to be right unless you do it exactly the way the boss wants it done, how likely are you to put in any extra effort? If you see something out of the ordinary, will you bring it to the forefront? Or will you push it down so you can get through the task without any additional hardship?

Consider a boss who rewrites literally every document their employees are responsible for, not just finding typos or making minor suggestions for changes, but completely rewriting them. No matter where you started the document, they'd have a completely different view of how it should go. It really didn't matter how good or bad the first take was; it wasn't their take and they couldn't see it any other way. And it wasn't just with you—it was with everyone on the team. It wasn't even predictable—their tastes seemed to be a moving target. Once you received their first round of comments and saw where they wanted it to go, though, things progressed more smoothly.

After a while of this, how much effort do you think team members would put into the first draft? The answer is, just enough to make it look like they tried. Why would they put a lot of effort into the first round when they knew it was going to get completely rewritten anyways? The boss already knew the answers, so why would you go out of your way to dig deeper on questions and bring new ideas to the table? That is not a healthy team dynamic.

Whether in the office, in the factory, or at home, the more you prescribe, the more you dictate, and the more you control, the more people will check out. The less you allow them to use their brains, the less they'll try.

People who show up just to clock in and out and receive a paycheck, by definition, will not be vigilant. They'll become the epitome of complacency: smug and overconfident with an inability to spot actual dangers or deficiencies. And they'll probably make you complacent in the process.

HOW TO DRIVE MORE ENGAGEMENT THROUGH AUTONOMY

How can we allow our employees and colleagues to be more autonomous and, therefore, more engaged? Here are six things you can do today to drive more engagement.

- **Focus on desired behaviors and outcomes rather than specific tasks**. Allow people to find their own routes to the destination where possible. As the saying goes, the journey is half the fun. If you find team members are hesitant to start down a path without getting your input first, it's likely they're just scared you already have a vision for how things should go, and they don't want to guess and have to redo things later. Create an environment that encourages, and rewards, taking those first steps on their own.

- **Ensure job performance measurements allow for flexibility**. If you only rate someone by how quickly they stock a shelf, they'll never make the choice to help a customer. Many call centers rate their representatives by how many calls they can take in a day. This forces them to try to keep each call's time down. Zappos, on the other hand, doesn't hold representatives to a call time metric. In fact, there's a story of one call that lasted nearly six hours! Look at what you use to measure success, and make sure those measurements focus on the results and behaviors you want to encourage and facilitate rather than handcuff (pun intended).

- **Design processes to include both shalls and mays.** Some things *must* be done a specific, prescribed way. Identify those, but make sure you allow for discretion in executing the ones that don't. Remember, a combination of the two still allows for the brain to work to differentiate between them and maintain engagement. Someone who commits domestic violence will have to go to jail. But I still need to determine the totality of the charges based on what I can discover and articulate. So, even in a case that seemingly has a lack of discretion, there's still a level of autonomy that keeps the brain working. If you've ever flown Southwest Airlines, you know that one of the distinct things about their flights is the safety announcement. We all know that every flight must start with a safety announcement, and generally, regardless of the airline, they're all pretty much the same. Most of the time, they're scripted to the word to make sure they meet the federal guidelines and get completed as quickly as possible. Some airlines have even taken these safety announcements completely out of the flight attendants' hands and have prerecorded them. But Southwest understands the beauty and benefit of autonomy. They allow their flight attendants to personalize the safety announcement. To make it their own. To be creative. To have fun. Of course, they *must* hit all the required points, but *the way* they do it is mostly up to them. They *shall* make the announcement, but they *may* insert their own personality. It's a great way to build engagement, and it doesn't hurt that the customers love it, too.

- **If you give the discretion, allow for the discretion**. There's nothing worse than making someone believe they have a choice, but then punishing them for not making the one *you* would've made. Allow for the fact that there are different paths to the same goals and embrace those differences. You may even learn something. For example, you can't tell an employee they can manage their own work schedule, using their discretion to decide when to be at the office and when to work from home, and then punish them for not being at the office when you are. The bait-and-switch is worse than no bait at all.

- **Provide timelines or deadlines and allow for check-in points. But allow the individual to decide how they proceed from check-in to check-in**. The points of review should be set up to catch any major issues or hurdles before they become a problem. The times in between, though, will allow the individual to feel a sense of ownership and control.

- **Let it go**. Ha-ha. Sorry for the ear worm. But it's true. Learn to let go. Micromanaging is just another way of saying you've removed the autonomy, the discretion, and, ultimately, the engagement. It's also a huge signal that you don't trust the person to complete the task on their own.

Remember, complacency can happen at any layer of an organization. The complacency that starts at the bottom and trickles to the top can be the hardest to unwind. Follow the steps above to ensure you foster autonomy and discretion wherever you can, and you'll generate the engagement that leads to the personal accountability and vigilance that protects against organizational complacency. And, if you can get a pizza along the way, all the better!

CHAPTER EIGHT VIGILANCE CHECK

Ask yourself:

1. How engaged are you in your work? How engaged are your employees or teammates?

2. How much autonomy do you/your employees/your teammates have? What are some opportunities to allow more discretion and autonomy?

3. Could the Zappos story about the pizza delivery from the customer service call happen at your organization? Why not?

4. Are you a micromanager? What are some opportunities for you to let it go?

CHAPTER NINE

—

Good Habits: Think Less for Increased Success

Return every phone call within 24 hours.

That was the rule that was dictated to me when I worked at Co-ca-Cola. I'm not even sure if it was a formal or informal rule. It didn't matter. It was important to whomever was writing my reviews and so it was important to me.

Notice the rule wasn't "return every phone call from our tier 1 customers within 24 hours." It was return *every* phone call within 24 hours. (Note that this was back in 1998. Robo-calling was not a thing yet. This rule now would probably be modified to "return every legitimate business phone call within 24 hours.")

I didn't think about the why too much at the time. I just knew I had to do it. And so, I did. I didn't think about whether a call was worth returning; I just returned it, even if it were just to say I had received the message and was working on a response.

What if the rule had been "return important calls within 24 hours"? That would have dictated that I evaluate each phone call before returning it. I would have to assign some level of importance to each one. Would I evaluate calls the same way as a colleague or my boss would? Would I be able to tell which ones were most important?

Perhaps I would assign importance by customer size. But that might overlook potential sales from currently small or new customers. Maybe I would assign importance by the relative urgency in the voice of the message-leaver. Maybe importance would be impacted by the plans I had that evening—the more enticing the plans, the less important the calls seemed. Maybe the more success I've been enjoying, the less I feel the need to return the calls immediately.

You get the point. One version of the rule removes all thought from the equation: You received a message; you return the call within 24 hours. No thinking; it's just a given. The other version allows for arbitrary thought, rationalizations, moving targets, and overconfidence.

In this situation, one version blocks complacency. The other invites it.

SEATING THE MAGAZINE (OR MAKING SURE THE THING THAT HOLDS THE BULLETS DOESN'T FALL OUT OF THE GUN)

Getting dressed for a shift involves a lot of steps when you're a uniformed police officer. You've got your clothes, obviously, but you also have all your extra stuff. Your badge and insignia. Your vest. Your duty belt. Your weapon(s). Your ammunition. Your handcuffs. Your flashlight(s). Your radio. Your earpiece. Your baton. Your tourniquet. Not to mention all the stuff that goes in your pockets: wallet, notebook, pens, business cards, duty gloves, medical gloves, evidence bags, and more. (Fun fact: By the time I've got my uniform, my boots, and all my gear on, I've packed on about 40 pounds of extra weight.)

Not only do you need to make sure you have everything, you also need to make sure it's all clean, presentable, and ready for action.

If you're in a rush, it's no small risk that you could miss something. Maybe it's a pen. That's ok. Maybe it's your gun. Not ok.

Specifically, on the gun, it's not enough to just have it—it needs to be in optimal working order. That means it must be clean and able to fire. It needs to be loaded. It needs to be set properly in your holster. Nothing on your belt can be in the way or hinder your draw. The magazine (the thing that holds the rounds) needs to be firmly seated with a round (bullet) in the chamber. If it's not, it will fall out as soon as you draw your gun from your holster. No es bueno.

That last bit about the magazine is pretty important. And you'd be surprised how easy it is to get it wrong.

Want to get laughed at on the range during qualifications or training? Draw your gun for an exercise with 15 other people on the line and watch your magazine go flying out of it. Not only will it fall out, but it will probably go a few feet in front of you—so everyone else there can watch as the firing must be stopped, and everyone must holster their weapon before you can sheepishly go retrieve it.

In training, it's embarrassing. In real life, it could be deadly.

So, every time I'm in the locker room getting dressed for a shift, the last thing I do is check to make sure the magazine in my gun is properly seated. I push on it and I give it a tug to make sure it doesn't come out. I don't even think about it. It's a habit that's instinctual. If it wasn't a habit, if I didn't do it every time without thinking about it, I might miss it occasionally. And the repercussions are just not worth the risk, regardless of how small it is.

TO THINK OR NOT TO THINK? THAT IS THE QUESTION

Consider this: Sometimes, thinking can get in the way of optimal decision-making. Other times, a lack of thinking can do the same thing. The trick is figuring out which is which and using habits and routines to ensure we keep them straight.

But, you might ask, aren't habits and routines the same thing? Nope. And the fundamental difference is all in your head. Literally.

According to Ann Graybiel's journal article "Habits, rituals, and the evaluative brain," habits are learned, pretty fixed, reliant on some triggering stimuli, and are "performed almost automatically, virtually nonconsciously, allowing attention to be focused elsewhere."[53]

In "Making health habitual: the psychology of 'habit-formation' and general practice" from the December 2012 edition of the *British Journal of General Practice*, the authors state that "…'habits' are defined as actions that are triggered automatically in response to contextual cues that have been associated with their performance…. Habits are also cognitively efficient, because the automation of common actions frees mental resources for other tasks."[54]

My habit of checking the seating of my magazine is triggered when I place my gun in my holster. It doesn't require any mental resources, because I don't even have to think about it.

Routines, on the other hand, require intentional thought. They require planning and deliberate action. They engage the mind.

Where habits are effortless, routines require effort. Think about it: They're called dance routines, not dance habits.

To simplify:

Habits remove thought from the equation.

Routines add thought back in.

Now, here's the complicated part. Complacency can weave its way into both habits and routines. And both habits and routines, when used properly, can help eliminate complacency.

Confused yet?

Let's break it down.

HABITS AND COMPLACENCY

For the purposes of this discussion, I want to go beyond the traditional definitions of good and bad habits. It's not just whether a habit is immediately beneficial (brushing teeth) or detrimental (smoking).

For me, a good habit is one that *decreases* overall risk or danger by eliminating thinking.

A bad habit is one that *increases* overall risk or danger by eliminating thinking.

Good habits can have a positive effect in the workplace and in your life. They can streamline low-level decisions, and provide structure and regimen. They can reinforce desired behaviors. And they take away the burden of *thinking*, because let's be honest, sometimes thinking just gets in the way.

What do you do with your keys when you walk in the house? If you're like me, the first thing you do is place them on the very same hook that's just inside the house. If you're like my wife (sorry babe), they could end up in one of several locations—the hook, the purse, the kitchen table, the upstairs bathroom (I will have to pay dearly for this story). Now, whose keys are most likely to go missing?

In this situation, I'm less likely than my wife to misplace my keys because I eliminate the thought. If I'm walking in the house with my keys, I put them on the hook. End of discussion.

If I allow myself to think about where I'm going to put the keys each time—and I decide on different locations based on what I'm doing, what time it is, or any other criteria—I increase the likelihood I'll put my keys in a spot I'll never remember. Thinking, in this case, increases the risk of losing (or misplacing for a while) my keys. By eliminating the thinking, I decrease (or eliminate) that risk.

By understanding this, we can then begin to look for situations in which we would benefit by removing thinking from the equation (i.e., where we can create a good habit). I have two important examples from law enforcement that will drive this home. And they both involve hands.

ELIMINATING THINKING TO CREATE A GOOD HABIT

Early in my career in law enforcement, I made a conscious decision to stop shaking hands. Most civilian people assume that it's because I'm a germaphobe. The truth is, the reason I stopped shaking hands revolves around officer safety and avoiding a dangerous habit.

I'm right-handed. So, when I reach out to shake someone's hand, I'm effectively giving up some control over my gun-side hand for a short period of time. To me, that doesn't make much sense. First, it puts me far too close to someone to be able to react optimally if the situation turned dangerous. Second, in the event things did take a turn for the worse, the opponent would already have a hold of my dominant hand.

Initially, it might seem overly paranoid to refuse handshakes to *everyone* in *every* situation. But to me, it makes perfect sense if you think of the alternative. If I'm not refusing handshakes with everyone, that means I must decide on a case-by-case basis whether this is a person I'm willing to shake hands with or not, which means I'd have to use some type of criteria.

Criteria might involve demographics, such as gender, size, age, physical appearance, manner of dress, etc. Maybe it would include information I may already have about that person's demeanor, attitude, or likelihood for violence. Maybe it would be situational, assigning different levels of threat based on whether the interaction was of a law enforcement nature or if it were more personal or business related. Maybe it would have something to do with my familiarity with the other person and how past interactions have gone.

Phew! That's a lot of things to potentially consider in the split second involved when someone offers their hand for a shake, right? And as we'll see in a later chapter, we're not necessarily good at making decisions when presented with a lot of data to consider.

You can see that the likelihood of making a wrong decision when faced with an outstretched hand could be high, especially if your default response is to shake the hand. Your hand might be heading out towards a shake before you even consciously know what's going on!

I recognize that the risk involved with each individual handshake (especially with those who look and act nonthreatening) is probably very low. In fact, most of those shakes (maybe all of them) will probably turn out just fine. Until one doesn't. And that's the rub, because the repercussions of getting that one wrong could be severe. This was driven home to me by one of my very first Field Training Officers. If I slip and offer my hand to someone, I can still feel his disapproving wince from over my shoulder. Of all the things that can get you booted from the Field Training program, lapses in officer safety are at the top of the list.

I quickly learned that, by leaving such a simple decision to be made in the moment, there are many ways the wrong decision can be made. Out of habit. Out of considering the wrong data. Out of misinterpreting the right data.

Recently, I worked swing shift for two nights in a row. On both those nights, I had interactions with the same person. The first night, I was working an active theft from a liquor store. Based on the description, I was able to find the thief. He was in possession of the liquor and readily admitted it was stolen. He wasn't particularly sorry about it, but he wasn't fighting us.

As another deputy wrote out his summons for a court appearance, the thief and I chatted. It was obvious there was some sort of drug problem or mental health issue (or both) in play, and I came to find out that he was homeless. I went to my patrol car and got my dinner out (sadly, it was a protein bar, a bag of chips, and a Gatorade). While we waited, I gave him the food and drink, which he quickly consumed before he went on his way (he refused a ride from us and just wanted to be done with us).

The next night, we were working a call about a disturbance at a convenience store that had turned into an assault. The suspect had fled the store on foot. Two other deputies caught up with him down the street. I arrived to provide backup and quickly recognized the guy as the same one from the previous night.

As you might imagine, I felt like we had a bit of a rapport at that point. I said hi to him, used his name, and reminded him who I was and how I had treated him the night before. He looked at me like I was an alien, and then he became, let's say, less compliant than the previous night. Getting him in a car was a struggle. He started spitting. Once we were at the jail, he tried to start a fight with another inmate. There was no recollection on his part of our previous interaction.

If we hadn't been in the middle of an assault call and I had just run into him on the street, it might be understandable if I had treated him like someone I knew. We had had a previous interaction. It was a calm and safe interaction. There might be the feeling of familiarity on my part. And, if I let those feelings impact whether I shake his hand, I might get punched in the face (or worse).

Here's a more common occurrence. I tend to give people a lot of warnings for low-level traffic infractions instead of writing them tickets or I write them lower-level tickets than their offense justified (i.e., I give them a break). People are generally appreciative of that gesture and display that through a gesture of their own—they offer their hands for a shake.

Without a habit that expressly prohibits it, I might be inclined to immediately reciprocate and complete the handshake. And now someone, in a vehicle that's currently running, has my hand. Perhaps I even reached into the car to complete the handshake and now I'm in even more potential danger.

Therefore, I decided my habit would simply be to not shake hands with anybody. My personal approach is the simple fist bump. When someone reaches out a hand, regardless of who it is, I smile and tell them I don't do handshakes. It's nothing personal, I tell them, just something I do with everyone. I might even tell them why. And I've never had a person get upset or offended by it.

By making that decision a habit, and by not trying to make individual decisions based on individual circumstances, I take my brain out of it. And I eliminate the possibility of making the wrong decision.

In this situation, taking thinking out of the decision lowers the risk of the decision. And the scenarios it addresses have the potential to carry very dangerous, even deadly, risks. This is exactly the situation that best lends itself to establishing a habit.

SHOW ME YOUR HANDS

Here's a second example involving the hands. Whenever I meet anyone in a law enforcement capacity, I ask them to keep their hands out of their pockets. No matter how routine the contact, how nice the person seems, how unlikely it is that they would have a weapon that they would be looking to deploy against me, I always ask them to keep their hands out of their pockets and where I can see them. It's hard for a lot of people, especially if it's cold out, they're anxious by nature, or they're on drugs. They pull their hands out of their pockets only to put them back 10 seconds later. And we go through it all again.

All police officers know that the hands are what can kill us. And we know we should keep people's hands visible and empty. But, unless you have an unwavering rule, it's easy to make a mistake. If you feel bad that the subject's hands might be cold, or you make the conscious decision that this encounter doesn't warrant it versus other encounters, you're bound to make a mistake that could prove fatal.

There's a specific video of an incident in Flagstaff, Arizona, from 2014.[55] Most police officers have probably viewed it and discussed it. It shows Flagstaff Police Officer Tyler Stewart being shot and killed during a domestic violence investigation. A college student had called to report her apartment being damaged after an argument with her boyfriend, Robert Smith. By the time police arrived, Smith had already left the apartment.

Officer Stewart then went to Smith's apartment to meet with him. Smith seems friendly and comes outside to chat, keeping his hands in his winter jacket pockets (it seems cold outside). Officer Stewart asks Smith if he has any weapons and Smith says he doesn't.

A little while into the conversation, you can tell from the camera (mounted on Officer Stewart's glasses) that Officer Stewart is becoming more concerned with Smith's hands. He asks Smith if he can pat him down. As he reaches to check Smith's pockets, Smith pulls out a gun and shoots Officer Stewart several times before shooting himself.

That video is a constant reminder to me, because, left to my own devices and subject to my own interpretations, I am 100 percent convinced I would make the wrong decision about someone at some point in my career (and probably at many points). In this situation, the original call to police indicated that the victim was not harmed physically but wanted to file a report because Smith had been yelling and caused damage to her apartment that she didn't want to be blamed for.[56] There was no mention of weapons. When Officer Stewart had originally taken the call, Smith had already left the scene.

Smith had later called police to calmly say that he had heard they were looking for him and to ask why. He was told a police officer would contact him. Officer Stewart was now trying to contact Smith at his own residence. It was no longer in the heat of the moment and there were no obvious indications that the meeting would be violent. By allowing for thinking, I might have made the same choices in the moment and also had the worst possible consequences.

Now, let's be clear—this is an extreme example. The risk and reward calculation doesn't need to get to the point of dangerous or deadly to justify a habit. It just has to be a situation where the safer choice is eliminating the thought, where the risks involved in deciding each iteration and getting even one wrong are great, and the risks involved in choosing the safe way every time are low.

WHERE COULD YOUR BUSINESS BENEFIT FROM LESS THINKING?

What processes or decisions in your business could benefit from removing the thinking? Find the elements that could potentially go the most wrong. Look for pieces of those that could be institutionalized. What are the things that are so dangerous that finding some easy ways to reduce the decision-making involved can help to ensure more consistently positive results?

Where are the situations where the potential downside of making the wrong decision is too great? Where are you more likely to make a mistake the more information you gather? Where are you likely to get complacent based on survivorship bias, even when you're not usually being punished directly or obviously for making the wrong decision? Those are the very best situations to develop good habits you can rely on.

In essence, what can you identify in your own business that's the equivalent of flossing after every meal, putting your keys in the same place every time, or always refraining from shaking hands?

If yours is a retail sales business, do you have a rule in place that everybody who walks in the door is treated with the same level of respect and friendliness? Or do you let employees decide based on their own criteria which customers might represent the most value?

Best-selling author and customer experience expert Shep Hyken (*The Cult of the Customer, Be Amazing or Go Home, The Convenience Revolution, Amaze Every Customer Every Time, The Amazement Revolution*) writes in a blog post about his experience at a car dealership when he was 22 years old.[57] He drove up to the showroom in his old clunker that had 170,000 miles on it. The salespeople saw him drive up and didn't give him the time of day, deciding he didn't have the means to buy one of their cars. The next day, he showed up again, but with his dad's much nicer car. He, predictably, received much more attention. He told the manager about the change in service between his two visits and was able to get a pretty good deal on a new car as an apology for the salespeople's behavior.

In this case, the cost of making the wrong decision based purely on aesthetics is way higher than the effort it takes to treat everyone as valuable. By allowing each individual salesperson to make their own decisions on potential customer value, how many wrong decisions might be made? Automate the decision—take the thought out of the process—and you won't guarantee a positive result (in terms of a sale), but you will guarantee that you'll avoid the embarrassing negative result of treating a potential customer rudely. It's a good habit to build, and it's also just the right thing to do!

You likely already use many habits in your workplace, and you can read numerous articles about great work habits to help you have a successful career. Habits like being on time, being able to take criticism, not gossiping, setting aside time to read every day, etc., are all things that you should do every time. They're meant to be part of who you are and how you act, without thinking about it.

The trick now is to take what you know about habits and apply them to the group, team, or organization level. What are the things you can do to increase success by removing the thought?

WHEN SHOULD YOU WRITE A BRIEF?

When you're in marketing, you become familiar with the concept of the creative brief. Say you're getting ready to put together an advertising campaign. Before the advertising agency can get started on the project, you would put together a creative brief.

The brief lays out the background, the goals, and the objectives of the campaign. It defines the positioning statement of the product or service, and it includes the target, the frame of reference, the brand promise, the benefits and features, and the reasons why people should believe all that. It defines the brand personality and attributes. It discusses the desired deliverables, and it defines the timeline and budget.

It's a useful and efficient tool. It's tells the creatives what success looks like and gives them the information to achieve it. And yet, often it's not really a habit, especially in smaller companies. It may be for *big* things, things that are going to cost a lot of money or take a long time. But its use can be hit-or-miss for the smaller things, because it takes time and energy and sometimes it feels unnecessary. And left to individual choice, it may not get done.

The creative brief, then, is something that can add significant value in terms of efficiency and quality of work product. There's no real downside to putting one together. It can only add to the clarity and consensus on success, which makes it a perfect candidate for becoming a habit.

Why not just decide that every project, big or small, is going to require a creative brief? Then there's no thought involved in terms of whether the project "deserves" it or not. If someone else is going to be expected to deliver on your expectations, you must lay out those expectations (and all the other helpful info) in a brief.

Maybe you're not in a role where creative briefs play a part. But what's your equivalent? What are the things that can provide benefit with very low risk? The things that could lead to negative results if they are not done? These are your opportunities for good corporate habits.

WHAT ABOUT BAD HABITS?

Unfortunately, the very reason that habits can yield positive results is also the reason that they can very quickly turn into a negative that creates the perfect storm for complacency to take hold.

We already know that habits can help eliminate thinking. However, when you're not actively thinking, you're not processing the stimuli around you. You're not taking notice of what might have changed from your expectations, therefore not paying attention to potential new dangers.

If someone (probably, after reading this, my wife) were to prank me and remove the hook that I normally place my keys on, the most likely result would be that the next time I walk into the house, I would promptly drop the keys directly onto the floor. I wouldn't notice that the hook wasn't there until it was too late. Because of my habit, I wouldn't actively receive new input as to what's going on around me before I make my motion with the keys. I wouldn't notice if anything has changed, because I wouldn't have a reason to.

Now, if, for some reason, we kept our expensive dinnerware on the floor beneath the key hook, this would be a very bad thing. It would also be a very stupid place to store expensive dishes, so we don't do that. But, if we did, dropping those keys would be a costly mistake.

We've seen that habits can be comforting, easy, and even lifesaving. But, on the flip side, they can also very quickly lead to complacency.

Remember, a key component of complacency is becoming *unaware* of actual dangers or deficiencies. Want to create the perfect environment for a lack of awareness? It's easy—just inhibit thinking. And in situations that bring with them significant risk, inhibition of thinking can be very damaging.

Here's a mild example. Not too long ago, I was rushing to get out of the house to get some errands done before I had to head to the airport to catch a flight. My truck was in the garage as always. I came out of the house, pressed the garage door opener, got in the truck, and threw it into reverse. Like I always do.

Except, this time the garage door had not opened. And I backed my truck right into a closed garage door, causing significant damage to the vehicle and the door. My habit was so ingrained, and I was in such a rush, that my brain didn't feel the need to gather any new information. It assumed everything was as it should be—but it wasn't.

Now, in the grand scheme of things, this wasn't a huge deal. I've got some battle scars on the back of my truck (which I don't care about—I think they add character!), and the garage door was able to get repaired that same morning (and I still made my flight!).

But what if the door was open and, for some crazy reason, a neighbor's child was standing right there? The consequences would obviously be far more severe.

Consider a factory where many workers are performing a series of tasks each day. Hundreds or thousands of times a day they may perform the same functions. It very quickly gets to the point where they can perform their jobs without thinking. You can imagine how dangerous a factory can be when people aren't thinking. And that's how workplace injuries take place.

Maybe you run a marketing team, and you always start a new project with some brainstorming. You always book the same conference room, invite the same people, and go through the same brainstorming techniques. In essence, you're going through the motions. And your creativity and inspiration suffer.

Perhaps you work in an office environment and your days are all very much the same. You arrive at a certain time, you get your coffee, you have your meeting, you run your reports, etc. You may also find yourself in a situation where much of what you're doing doesn't require a lot of thinking. Just like when you're driving your car and suddenly realize you can't remember how exactly you got from point A to point B, you may get to lunchtime in the office and not even know how you got there.

And that's how you miss things. Information. Personal cues from coworkers. Maybe even data within the reports you're running. The consequences could vary from nonexistent to mild to catastrophic.

Even good habits can create dangerous situations. Maybe I create a habit that at the start of every shift, I walk around the police car and check to make sure all the lights work. That habit can be a useful way of ensuring I don't rush into service with a vehicle that has a defect. Believe me, it's no fun pulling someone over for not using their signal and then realizing your own is on the fritz!

However, that habit at the start of a shift can become dangerous. If I get so ingrained in checking the lights and the car as I walk around it that I lose situational awareness of what's happening around me, I can become vulnerable to an ambush, especially if someone has been watching me and identifying my habits. If I'm not careful, I can go so far into autopilot that I stop paying attention to the stimuli and new information available around me. Unaware of potential dangers. Complacent.

As I mentioned earlier in the book, law enforcement work is sometimes described as 99 percent mundane and 1 percent insane. I'd venture to guess many people's jobs are just like that. The problem is that, if you're not careful, the 99 percent mundane can lead to shutting off thinking in the most inopportune times.

When you have a habit that's moving from helpful (or, at least, benign) to dangerous, you'll likely see obvious signs—if you're paying attention. I like to call those signs "mini-phew" moments. We've all had them, the close calls that make your heart stop a little or make the hairs on your arms stand at attention.

I just mentioned how you can drive all the way home and not remember how you get there because you were on autopilot. Phew. Or you were backing out of a parking spot and almost got into an accident. Phew. Or you created an enormous spreadsheet and almost forget to hit Save. Phew. Maybe they all turn out ok, this time. But for a moment, you were pretty scared.

If you're not paying attention, you might have your moment of panic and then go back to business as usual. But if you pay attention to those mini-phews and see them for what they are, you can use them to instigate a change to the process, an insertion of conscious thought to disrupt the nonconscious habit.

So, what do we do once we identify a bad habit?

IMPROVE THE HABIT, TURN IT INTO A ROUTINE, OR DISRUPT IT COMPLETELY

In some situations, a bad habit can be changed into a good one. These are situations where it's just the habit itself that's detrimental, and if you can change a key element or two, you can move it to the win column.

Take smoking, for example. Maybe you have certain triggers that lead you to a cigarette, like a time of day, a meal, a stressful event, or a social occurrence. If you can replace the cigarette with something else—chewing a piece of gum, flicking a rubber band, eating a lollipop—you can shift the habit from bad to good (or at least better) and still not require thinking. Listen, I know quitting smoking is not that easy; changing habits never is. But if you could, I think we would agree it would be good.

In the office, maybe you've noticed a habit of scheduling meetings every time something needs to be discussed. The default time for the meeting requests is one hour. Because of a general tendency to fill allotted time, the meetings are not as productive as they could be.

The result is a lot of wasted time and calendars that are always full of meetings. What if, though, you changed the default meeting time to 15 minutes? You could always increase it for meetings that truly require it but think of all the time you could free up. By making one small change, you've changed a bad habit into a good one.

In some situations, though, the habit is bad because it has eliminated thinking that would be beneficial to have. It has automated things that could really benefit from conscious thought. In those situations, you need to transform the bad *habit* into a good *routine* by inserting intention and deliberate actions that actively involve thought. You need to eliminate the root of the complacency.

Consider the brainstorming issue earlier. What if you didn't always have it in the same conference room? What if you moved locations? What if you got your team on a train and did the brainstorming while traveling? What if you took the team offsite—to anywhere, really—where new stimuli could be introduced? What if you invited different people, people not even on your team or working in your department? What if you still did a brainstorming session to start every project, but you did it differently each time?

Now you've created a routine instead of a habit.

Consider my story earlier of backing the truck into the garage. Once I realized I had a bad habit, I changed it to a good routine. I inserted specific and intentional moments for active observance and stimuli acceptance. I make sure the garage is completely up, and I look behind the truck and around the area to see who's out and about *before* getting in the driver's seat. I then purposefully look in my mirrors and consciously record what I see before putting the truck in reverse and backing up.

Sometimes, though, you may find that you can't successfully break a habit by turning it into a routine. The risks may be too great, and the situation is just too conducive to complacency. In those situations, you may have to actively disrupt the habit to force thought and make sure outside information is being processed.

Consider the warehouse or factory floor scenario. The work may be repetitive, and it may be easy to fall into bad habits that involve not thinking and not paying attention to the potential dangers all around.

In a situation like this, you'll need to actively disrupt the habits using reminders: visual signs ("DANGER!" or "Wash Your Hands" or "X Days Since Last Accident"), audible alerts (like a beeping sound on a forklift), checklists (like a pilot might use for takeoff and landing), and tactile prompts (like the rumble strips that let you know when your vehicle is drifting out of its lane).

Use whatever works. Just find the places and times that are most susceptible to the formation of damaging routines or the lapse of good routines, and then insert something—anything—that forces conscious thought. Bring the brain back into the equation. Minimize the risk of ignoring or missing the signs of potential threats or danger and minimize the probability of complacency.

You can see how this is incredibly important in workplaces where real physical danger exists. But it's also relevant to jobs with fewer physical risks.

Say your job involves email marketing. You're the one who puts together and sends out marketing, promotional, and other emails to your customers and potential customers. You do this every day. Designing, coding, scheduling, and sending. It's easy to get into habits that can eliminate thought, but the risks if mistakes are made can be substantial. Grammatical errors, spelling mistakes, link problems, or any other errors can lead to decreased click-throughs, customer dissatisfaction, or worse, unsubscribes. Even more problematic could be sending perfectly crafted emails to the wrong lists.

This is a perfect scenario for adding in stimuli to actively disrupt the repetition of the tasks. It could be signage, a checklist, some automated prompt, or even a system function that takes over. Or a combination of those. Use anything to wake the mind up, refocus it, and make sure big mistakes don't happen due to repetition, lack of thought, and complacency.

TO THINK OR NOT TO THINK...

Remember, the difference between a habit and a routine is all in your head. First identify the places in your day, in your week, in your life where you can safely improve your performance by eliminating thought. This is where you can create or encourage good habits.

Then identify the places where you are *unsafely* eliminating thought. Consider if you can turn those bad habits into good ones. If not, determine what level of conscious thought, deliberate action, or intentional behavior can mitigate the risks and create more successful outcomes, thereby creating good *routines* out of bad habits.

And, when all else fails, disrupt, disrupt, disrupt.

CHAPTER NINE VIGILANCE CHECK

Ask yourself:

1. Where can your business benefit from *less* thinking?

2. What bad habits currently exist that could benefit from the reintroduction of thought?

3. What are processes or tasks within your business that could benefit from active disruption to ensure complacency doesn't settle in?

CHAPTER TEN

──────

Accountability + Transparency = Vigilance: The ATV Model

In these times, seeing is believing, and the assumption is that things that can't be seen are probably being hidden. Proceed without transparency at your own peril. You've been warned.

It's no secret that the public's trust in nearly everything has been declining. In August 2020, for example, a Gallup survey showed that confidence in the police had dropped to an all-time low at 48 percent.[58]

The picture's even worse for the federal government. According to a Pew Research Center survey conducted July 23 through August 4, 2020, "[j]ust 20 percent of US adults say they trust the government in Washington to 'do the right thing' just about always or most of the time."[59] Contrast this to 1964, when the American National Election Study showed that 77 percent of respondents trusted the federal government to do the right thing.[60]

But lack of trust isn't just a government thing (according to the 2020 Edelman Trust Barometer that came out in January 2020). Public confidence in corporations is at only 58 percent.[61] I think we can agree that even though it looks high versus public confidence in the government, it's not a number that we should be proud of.

Imagine walking into a local appliance store in the 1960s. You see the salesperson, and you're happy they're walking over. You probably know them. You like them. You trust them. The interaction is easy and helpful.

Contrast that with the feeling you get today when you realize a salesperson is coming up to you, unsolicited, in a retail store or car dealership. Be honest. Do you have a feeling of ease and trust? Or do you immediately go on the defensive and protect your wallet? Or run away?

How about answering the phone? How often do you pick up when it's from a number you don't recognize? Admit it; if you do pick up, it's sometimes just because you feel like trying to mess with a scammer!

So, we can probably agree that trust has declined significantly over the years. One of the manifestations of that declining trust is that the assumption about many social, governmental, and financial transactions is that the other party has bad intent. Our guards are naturally up. We expect the worst from people, governments, and companies.

And that feeling is exacerbated when we feel like we're being lied to or if we feel that information is being withheld. If someone isn't giving me the whole story, they must be lying to me, right? And if they're lying to me, it must be for evil reasons. It's the only logical conclusion.

LACK OF TRUST REMOVES THE BENEFIT OF THE DOUBT

If the underlying assumption is that the other party has bad intentions, then it's logical that anything hidden or undisclosed will be viewed in the most negative light possible.

There are few more flammable situations today than when a negative incident with law enforcement occurs and there is no body camera footage. It doesn't matter the reason given as to why there isn't any footage. Maybe the department hasn't issued its officers body cameras, or the camera fell off the uniform during a foot pursuit or scuffle (body cameras are usually attached to the uniform with a magnet), or the body camera required manual activation and the officer failed to do so in the heat of the moment.

The reasons don't much matter to those who already have a natural distrust or distaste for the police. Their natural conclusion will likely be that the lack of body camera footage stems from a desire or need to hide damning information from the public. The assumption will often be that it's representative of a cover-up and is an indication of guilt.

For someone already in that mindset, the conclusions are clear. The benefit of doubt, in their minds, has not been earned and will not be given.

In August 2020, the Chicago police's shooting of a Black man "… prompted hundreds of vandals to descend on the city's famed Magnificent Mile shopping area, where they smashed store windows and made off with everything from clothing to cash registers."[62] The police said that the man had fired at them first, but the officers involved had not been issued body cameras. Video obtained from a surveillance camera in the neighborhood was inconclusive.

Chicago has a long history of distrust between the community and its police force. In at least one previous incident, a special unit was disbanded "…after an investigation revealed members were robbing drug dealers and committing home invasions and other crimes."[63]

After the August 2020 shooting, "activists immediately seized on the news that the officers were not wearing body cameras (and) issued a statement questioning the department's version of events. 'These details are uncorroborated, partially because CPD also claims there is no body camera footage available for this interaction,' the group said."[64]

Because the community and activists were already skeptical, there was a tendency to distrust what they could not see. The police version of events wasn't enough without the body camera footage. And the lack of the footage just reinforced the lack of trust. The lack of transparency may even have led to the assumption that it was purposeful and meant to hide transgressions.

These assumptions have even been codified into law. In June 2020, on the heels of the killings of George Floyd (a 46-year-old Black man killed by police in Minneapolis) and Elijah McClain (a 23-year-old Black man who died during an interaction with Aurora, Colorado, police and firefighters),[65] Colorado was the first state to pass a bill aimed at law enforcement reform.[66]

Among other things, the bill specifically states that if body cameras or dash cameras aren't activated as required, "there is a permissive inference in any investigation or legal proceeding…that the missing footage would have reflected misconduct by the Peace Officer." It goes on to say that any statements that weren't captured on camera can be deemed inadmissible in court.

In essence, if a peace officer in the state of Colorado fails to activate their BWC (body-worn camera) for *any* reason (other than equipment malfunction), the assumption is that the peace officer was up to no good. So, in Colorado, the officer's word is no longer good enough. What wasn't recorded is seen in the worst possible light for the officer.

Many other states and municipalities either already have body camera legislation or are considering it. In November 2020, the state of New Jersey passed bill NJ S1163, which requires law enforcement officers to wear body cameras. As of this writing, Virginia has a similarly focused bill (VA HB5135) that's still in committee.[67]

When trust disappears, so does the benefit of the doubt. In that type of environment, transparency is not just nice to have. It's a requirement.

WHAT DOES THIS HAVE TO DO WITH COMPLACENCY?

A lack of accountability and transparency, combined with power, can easily result in the overconfidence and self-satisfaction that can lead to complacency. If nobody is watching and things are going smoothly, you could easily be lulled into the self-satisfaction that blinds you from lurking dangers or threats.

The 58 percent public confidence in corporations is the result of corporate complacency, and the results can be disastrous. Consider the financial crisis of 2008, during which a lack of transparency resulted in a lack of confidence that all but crippled the financial system of the United States.

As a quick refresher, deregulation in the banking industry at the time led to a laxer environment with less oversight, which allowed banks to take on riskier endeavors in the mortgage space than they would have previously.[68] Due to low interest rates, they were able to sell a lot of mortgages and then lay off the risk by bundling those mortgages and reselling them. The people who bought the bundles then divided them up and resold them again. Due to a lack of transparency, the further down the line you were, the less likely you were to know how much risk you were actually buying.

Since banks had plenty of money to lend, they sought to write more and more mortgages, relaxing the criteria for the loans along the way until they were eventually writing very risky loans to people who couldn't afford them and didn't really understand what they were signing up for. This was all fine, as long as the market remained favorable—which, of course, it did not.

Eventually the interest rates went up, and that large number of people who had no idea what they had signed up for suddenly had much higher payments when their mortgage rates adjusted. People started defaulting. At the same time, the housing market crashed, and the mortgage holders couldn't sell the houses they were now foreclosing on.

The fact that low-risk investments had just become high-risk investments led to a lot of confusion and uncertainty. As a result, banks stopped lending to each other, opting to keep the cash for their own day-to-day survival.

Lehman Brothers, one of the world's biggest financial institutions, went bankrupt. Bear Stearns was rescued by JPMorgan for $2 a share.[69] There was worry that ATMs would run out of money. Millions of homes were foreclosed on. It was a mess. It required massive government bailouts (and as a result, increased regulation). And many would say it was, in a large part, due to a lack of transparency.

Uncertainty leads to fear. Fear leads to panic. Panic leads to suboptimal decisions. All the while, trust is eroded so much that even when information is forthcoming, it isn't believed.

The lack of transparency that led to the financial crisis of 2009 was a bad combination with the power of large banking institutions. The success they were experiencing allowed them to ignore the potential risks—until they could not ignore them anymore.

As a result of the financial crisis of 2008, several legislative actions were taken. The most significant was the Dodd-Frank Wall Street Reform and Consumer Protection Act, which further regulated the financial services industry. In doing so, it created several new agencies tasked with keeping watch over the industry, like the Financial Stability Oversight Council (FSOC) and the Consumer Financial Protection Bureau (CFPB). The act also served to provide protections for whistleblowers.[70]

The only way to rebuild trust is through accountability and transparency. The financial crisis of 2008 lasted until June 2009 and then the rebuilding began. In 2012, the financial services and banking industries were still suffering the effects of the financial crisis and were the "least trusted industries in the world" at 44 percent.[71] By May 2020, the financial services industry had reached an all-time high in trust at 64 percent.[72]

SCATHING REVIEWS AND BOYCOTTS: THE BACKLASH ON FACEBOOK'S LACK OF ACCOUNTABILITY

Consider Facebook and its historic lack of accountability and transparency. What started in a college dorm room quickly became a behemoth with the power of a nation (or several). The social media site has over 2.6 billion active users as of the first quarter of 2020, making it the largest in the world.[73] Facebook also owns Instagram and WhatsApp, two of the other biggest social media sites in the world.[74]

Facebook, of course, makes its money by selling ads. The primary benefit it provides when it sells ads is that the user data it has allows the ads to be highly targeted.[75] The use of that data has, in recent years, created larger and larger stirs regarding privacy and political influence.

I'm sure you've noticed that Facebook (and many other sites) can place very creepy, incredibly targeted ads in your feeds. Seth Stephens-Davidowitz is the author of *Everybody Lies: Big Data, New Data, and What the Internet Can Tell Us About Who We Really Are.* On March 29, 2018, Stephens-Davidowitz wrote the following tweet on his Twitter account (@SethS_D):

> *I just got a Facebook ad for hair loss product. Are they using my pictures to figure out I am balding? I am pretty sure there is no other way, using my internet behavior, for them to know that.*[76]

Not only can Facebook target ads based on your demographics, but they can also calculate things that might interest you based on your posts or your emotions. They can allow advertisers to load up email lists of customers and then, if you seem like those people, add you to the mix. They can see what things you're shopping for if you're doing it while logged into Facebook, and then target ads to you based on that observed behavior.

You can see how all of this would be extremely enticing to Facebook. The more users they have and the more they know about them, the more ads they can sell and the more they can charge for those ads.

The business proposition from a dollars-and-cents standpoint is clear. The lack of legislation and competition removes most external barriers that would prevent them from doing this. And so, they did it. Big time.

But then issues started bubbling to the surface. Big issues. Visible and public issues.

In 2018, there was the Cambridge Analytica scandal, where "Facebook permitted the 'unfair' sharing of user data with developers without 'clear and informed consent,' according to regulators. Up to 87 million users in the UK, US, and beyond are believed to have been affected. User data, including names, liked content, and locations, may have been used to sway voters in the lead to the US presidential elections."[77]

This was followed by a series of other accusations regarding Facebook's complicity in incidents related to outside interests trying to influence the United States' political elections.

As Natasha Lomas wrote in her TechCrunch article "Facebook data misuse and vote manipulation back in the frame with latest Cambridge Analytica leaks":

Platforms whose profiteering purpose is to track and target people at global scale—which function by leveraging an asymmetrical "attention economy"—have zero incentive to change or have change imposed upon them. Not when the propaganda-as-a-service business remains in such high demand, whether for selling actual things like bars of soap, or for hawking ideas with a far darker purpose.[78]

It seems that because they *can*, they do.

Recently, the United States government has taken a keen interest in Facebook and other large social platforms. It's clear that regulation is on their minds.

Additionally, in the summer of 2020, more than 1,000 companies publicly joined a boycott of ad buying. Calling it #StopHateFor-Profit, the companies were protesting how Facebook handles (or fails to handle) hate speech and misinformation in general. Nine companies in particular cut nearly $26 million in total from their Facebook ad buys.[79]

Combine this with some troubling consumer usage numbers, and the signals become clear. According to the Infinite Dial 2020 report from Edison Research and Triton Digital, only 32 percent of people in the United States aged 12 to 34 report that Facebook is the social network they use most often, down from 58 percent in 2015. Comparatively, Instagram is reported as most used by 27 percent in that same age group, up from 15 percent in 2015.[80]

Facebook's declines are not surprising. According to a March 2019 NBC News/*Wall Street Journal* poll, 60 percent of those surveyed said that they don't trust Facebook to protect their personal information *at all*. Another 32 percent said they had some trust in Facebook. Only a total of 6 percent said they trusted Facebook with their personal data either quite a bit or a lot.[81]

Without accountability or transparency, vigilance is inhibited. Eventually, hubris and power can lead to complacency. And complacency is, eventually, a self-correcting problem. Trust erodes. Sooner or later (probably sooner), a threat will emerge that will be underestimated (or missed altogether). Whether it is government intervention, a new competitive entry, or just customer attrition, it will come. And when it does, the customer will be more than ready for it. Counting on customers staying with you because there aren't any other suitable options is never a good long-term strategy.

TRANSPARENCY AS A CHECK ON POWER

"The true test of a man's character is what he does when no one is watching," is a quote attributed to John Wooden, legendary UCLA basketball coach.[82]

This is a great quote, and one I use with my daughters (although I change the pronouns). The quote reflects a fantastic ideal that I believe everyone should try to live up to: do good because it's the right thing to do, not because you're being watched.

But like most easy, pithy quotes, it lives in a binary world of all or nothing, a world most of us don't live in.

In the real world, not every decision feels like a character test. And without oversight (internal or external), it's easy to fall into small traps that can lead to bigger mistakes down the road.

A multiplying effect is the involvement of power. The more power someone has, the freer rein they are given without consequences, and the more they can convince themselves that what they're doing is right and just. This happens not just at the big corporate level, like in the financial crisis discussed previously, but all the way down to the personal level. We can talk about the abuse of power at the macro–corporate and government levels, but the reality is that it all starts with individual ordinary people.

Without reason to question ourselves, how far down the wrong path can we get before we realize it? And, once we've gone down that path too far, does it end up looking like the right path to us because it's now so familiar?

Consider these two situations—are they equal?

First, a police officer is in line at a coffee shop. They get up to the front of the line and order. The person behind them gets the cashier's attention and says they'd like to pay for the officer's coffee. The officer tells them thank you but it's not necessary. The citizen insists, pays for the coffee, and thanks the officer for their service.

Second, a police officer orders their coffee and asks the cashier if the store gives free coffee to officers. It normally doesn't, but the cashier feels awkward and gives the officer the coffee for free.

It's just a cup of coffee, right? The coffee is the same. But one of these is a pleasant and innocent interaction, and the other is an abuse of power. The line can become blurry for some, but even the smallest infraction should be avoided. If not, you're heading down a slippery slope.

Think about wining and dining in business. At what point does it move from a friendly gesture to a bribe? In the pharmaceutical industry, things became muddy enough that, to avoid a "regulatory crackdown, drug makers adopted a voluntary code of conduct in 2009 that, among other restrictions, permits only 'modest, occasional meals' in 'appropriate circumstances,' facilitating 'the exchange of medical and scientific information.' Though this curbed the most ridiculous excesses…research shows that even a $20 lunch can sway prescribing behavior."[83]

HOW FRICTION HELPS AVOID SLIPPERY SLOPES

Have you ever played on a Slip 'N Slide? The original one was introduced by Wham-O back in 1961, so you'd have to be trying hard to have avoided one all these years.[84] If you're not familiar, though, it's basically a long sheet of plastic you connect to a hose. The water from the hose comes out of small perforations on the side and sprays out onto the sheet, making it very slippery and tons of fun on a hot day. Lucky enough to have a small hill in your backyard? Oh boy!

Why do Slip 'N Slides work so well? Gravity, inertia, momentum all come into play (especially when on a slope). Lack of friction is also a major factor. In fact, some people will add lubricating liquids to the slide to further remove friction and allow for a more slippery slide.

Likewise, when abuses of power occur, inertia, momentum, and lack of friction can often be found in the mix. In law enforcement, far before any abuses of power become extreme, there are usually warning signs. These small abuses of power may not amount to anything criminal but are perched at the top of a very slippery slope.

Unfortunately, these small abuses can often result in positive outcomes for the officer. When this happens, it reinforces the feelings of power and invincibility that lead to overconfidence, which leads to complacency and the lack of awareness or recognition of existing dangers and risks. This complacency can lead to further negative actions being taken down the road. And, beyond the devastating damage this can do to the citizens directly involved in the incidents, it can also breed a general negative feeling about law enforcement from the public.

The lack of negative repercussions from colleagues or superiors basically adds lubrication to the slide, making it that much more slippery and that much harder to stop. The hardest part is that the individual may not even think they are doing wrong. They might perceive it as they're getting what they deserve, what they worked for, and what others owe them.

Transparency, oftentimes, can add the friction that is so desperately needed. It can provide the element that forces the self-reflection and self-examination that can lead to vigilance. That friction, though, will not introduce itself. It needs to be formalized and publicized—internally and externally.

THE ATV MODEL: ACCOUNTABILITY REQUIRES TRANSPARENCY, AND VIGILANCE IS THE RESULT

The public doesn't demand transparency from companies so they can read reports. And they don't demand transparency from law enforcement for the sake of being able to watch videos. They do it to achieve *accountability*, the obligation or willingness to accept responsibility for one's actions.

Just the sheer introduction of accountability forces those being held accountable (or holding themselves accountable) to pay more attention to what they're doing, to think through the consequences, and to evaluate options and choose the optimal paths. By increasing awareness and forcing stimulus analysis and conscious decision-making, we increase our ability to remain vigilant and therefore avoid complacency.

When banks know they're being scrutinized by government agencies, by the media, and ultimately by the public, and that they're going to be held accountable for their actions, they're naturally more vigilant about those actions. When Facebook must disclose how they're using your data, they naturally become more vigilant about using it properly.

We've already talked about body cameras. When a law enforcement agency writes a body camera policy, announces publicly that they'll be using body cameras and releasing the footage within certain timeframes and rules, and outfits their officers with the cameras, they've put a stake in the ground for all to see. They're letting people know that they'll be held accountable. Not only does the public know it, but the officers know it as well.

Most agencies won't outwardly talk about any behavior changes that come about by wearing a body camera, and the few studies that have looked at the effectiveness of body cameras have focused on statistics such as arrests, complaints lodged, and uses of force—not on officer attitudes or behaviors.

But a study of body cameras conducted with the Phoenix Police Department in 2014 found that complaints against the officers who wore body cameras decreased by 23 percent versus a 10.6 percent *increase* in complaints against the officers in the same precinct who didn't wear them and a 45.1 percent increase for officers in other precincts.[85]

A separate study with the Las Vegas Police Department found that "BWC-wearing officers generated significantly fewer complaints and use of force reports relative to control officers without cameras."[86]

While these significant drops in complaints and use of force could be related to several different factors, anyone who's ever been recorded knows that you can't help but be affected just by knowing that the recording is taking place.

Some law enforcement agencies are going further towards establishing more accountability and transparency. In the wake of a series of police use-of-force controversies in 2020, several cities around the US moved to create civilian review boards to provide outside oversight to agencies and combat the fear that police couldn't be trusted to police themselves.

In November 2020, the Metro Council of the City of Louisville, Kentucky, voted 25–1 to approve the creation of a civilian review board. Mayor Greg Fischer said, "This new system of independent review will provide an extra layer of police accountability and is an integral component to the work we're doing to rebuild community trust and legitimacy between @LMPD (Louisville Metro Police Department) and those they serve."[87]

On Election Day 2020 NBC News reported that police reform legislation had been approved in at least six states, "reflecting a growing demand for greater law enforcement accountability." In municipalities in four other states—California, Texas, Oregon, and Ohio—measures passed that "approved creating, overhauling or strengthening police oversight boards." Portland's measure not only created a committee that could investigate police misconduct and uses of deadly force, but "would also have the power to discipline officers for wrongdoing."[88]

Civilian review boards are not a new invention. New York City has had some form of one since 1953.[89] While there's very little information about the overall effectiveness of civilian review boards in enacting meaningful change due to the wide inconsistencies in how they're set up, what their powers are, who they report to, etc., a 2018 study on civilian oversight commissioned by the Department of Justice showed consistency in their objectives:[90]

- Transparency

- Independent investigations

- Improving accountability

- Improving public trust and legitimacy

- Engaging the community

- Demystifying police internal affairs investigations

So, while time will tell if review boards have a significant impact on the way police agencies conduct their business, it's clear that the objectives of accountability and transparency will continue to drive the pursuit.

To provide accountability, we must provide transparency, which leads to vigilance and ultimately combats complacency. I call this the ATV model (Accountability, Transparency, Vigilance).

Consider this quick example. You decide you want to lose weight, and so you start counting your calories and getting on the scale. You write your goals down in a journal. This personal *accountability* (deciding to set a goal and write it down) requires internal *transparency* (recording calories and weight versus goals in the journal), which leads to *vigilance* (seeing your daily progress, or lack thereof, pushes greater compliance).

Now, let's take things up a notch. Say that instead of just writing down your health goals, you post them to social media. Now you're not only accountable to yourself but also to your friends, family, coworkers, etc.

In doing so, you've created a system that requires transparency. If these people are going to hold you accountable, they must have information that conveys progress. And which is going to be more powerful and believable—something you write or a picture you show? There's a reason every diet and fitness product on the market utilizes before and after photos for their advertisements. As I stated at the start of this chapter, seeing is believing.

Now, to close the loop, what does the increase in transparency do? It increases your vigilance! Knowing that other people are watching (and looking for pictures) and being accountable to those other than yourself increases the chances you'll make the behavior changes required to deliver on the commitment. This is the hidden benefit of transparency.

Accountability is the goal. Transparency is the tactic. Vigilance is the byproduct: ATV.

CREATE YOUR OWN TRANSPARENCY BEFORE SOMEONE ELSE DOES

If you find yourself or your organization somewhere along the slippery slope of power abuse, it's more than likely it can be at least partly traced back to a lack of oversight, a lack of accountability, and a lack of transparency. If that's the case, it's up to you to bring that accountability, transparency, and self-evaluation into your world before someone else does it for you.

Accountability and transparency were forced on the banking industry after the financial crisis of 2008.

Facebook didn't pay much attention to changing their ways until the advertiser boycotts and government interest.

Even though police car dash cameras have been around since the 1980s and body-worn cameras have been around in law enforcement since around 2005, the focus on cameras in policing didn't really pick up steam in the United States until 2014, following the shooting death of Michael Brown by a police officer in Ferguson, Missouri.[91]

There are those agencies, though, that didn't adopt BWC policies. They're now the most vulnerable to criticism, especially when things go wrong. They're the agencies that get accused of hiding things, of incubating corrupt mindsets, and of requiring the most outside intervention to ensure accountability. You should learn from these mistakes. If there are opportunities for increased transparency in your business, pursue them now. Waiting for someone else to make you is never the best look.

Here are some suggestions for how to find areas that could benefit from increased transparency:

- **Find where the most misinformation lies**. Misinformation generally evolves from information gaps. The easiest way to solve it is to close those gaps. Ask yourself why those gaps exist in the first place. If people are filling in the holes, they must be interested. You may find that you just assumed people knew. Or you may find that you *were* trying to hide (or at least avoid) information. You may even find that competitors are exploiting the information gaps and people's natural level of distrust to create false narratives.

Whatever the source of the problem, the best approach is to address it head-on. If you *are* essentially hiding information because you're ashamed or scared for others to know the truth, what can you do to either effect a meaningful change or at least explain openly why things are the way they are? If you've just been omitting the information because you thought it was irrelevant, realize it *is* relevant and start providing it. If someone is just plain making things up, get out in front of it.

It's never going to be the best option to let your constituents decide on their own why the information they want isn't coming from you. The assumption will nearly always be the worst possible interpretation.

In order to successfully combat misinformation, though, you must do it quickly. Learn from the experience of the social app Houseparty. When the coronavirus lockdowns began around the world in the beginning of 2020, Houseparty was poised to be one of the big winners. Downloads spiked. In the first week of March 2020, the app was downloaded about 2 million times, compared to just 130,000 downloads in the same week one month earlier. At the time, it held the number 1 ranking in the Apple store across 17 countries.[92]

In March, however, rumors started on Twitter that hackers were entering users' other accounts through a Houseparty security flaw. Houseparty maintained that the news was fake and quickly worked to get in front of the bad information. In a March 30, 2020, tweet, they even offered a hefty ($1,000,000) reward to the first person who could prove that a "commercial smear campaign" was taking place.[93]

Nobody claimed the reward. But neither did anyone come forward to prove there was an actual security flaw. Houseparty didn't run and hide from the danger. They addressed it head-on and showed a real confidence in their truth.

The rumor mill calmed down and eventually all but disappeared. A potential disaster was averted. In an April 15, 2020, article, Houseparty co-founder and CEO Sima Sistani reported that the app had seen 50 million signups in the past month.[94]

- **Show your cards. Open the doors. Give a peak under the hood. Pull back the curtain. Whatever analogy you want to use, let people see what's actually going on in your operation.** Find out what piques people's curiosity about your business and then answer that curiosity. Let diners see your kitchen. Invite your customers into your manufacturing facilities. Provide a live webcam of your operations. In law enforcement, we do ride-alongs. Be honest and open and don't provide any indication you're hiding something.

As I've mentioned, I run an annual marketing conference called Brand ManageCamp (https://BrandManageCamp.com). After 17 years of hosting the conference live (more than half of those in Las Vegas), on came the coronavirus pandemic of 2020. Obviously, live events ground to a halt. We had to figure something out.

We quickly moved the event to a virtual format, working with all of our speakers to design an event that was not just a three-day webinar, but was custom fit for adult online learning behavior and was optimized to deliver actionable insights in a way that fit the new paradigm of work.

We decided that the best way to allow our speakers to do what they do best while avoiding any potential technical glitches was to have them prerecord their sessions to be livestreamed during our event. We would broadcast the sessions and then bring the speakers on live afterwards for Q&A.

To be honest, the first line of thought was, "How are we going to maintain the illusion of being live?" We initially asked the speakers to plan on matching their outfits that they wore during their videos when they appeared live for the Q&A to further the narrative that everything was happening live. We feared that if attendees knew everything was prerecorded, they would find less value in the experience.

This line of thought was very short-lived. I very quickly realized that what we were talking about doing amounted to lying to the people who were most valuable to us. There was no world I could imagine where that was the best course of action.

Instead, we were upfront and honest with our attendees. We told them that all the sessions were prerecorded. We explained why that decision was made. We leveraged this honesty to be able to provide additional value. Each speaker attended the conference live and interacted with the attendees via chat *while* their sessions were being aired. Attendees were able to ask questions and give reactions in real time, and they were able to get an immediate response directly from the expert.

When their sessions ended, we brought each speaker into

our live video Q&A where we continued the discussion.

Attendees *loved* it. In their reviews of the event, they confessed they were a bit concerned when they learned the sessions were prerecorded. But once they got started, they realized how valuable the increased interaction with the speakers was and the whole thing just felt comfortable.

Can you imagine what would have happened if we had tried to pull off the charade? Inevitably, people would have figured out the lie. And the trust we had worked so hard to build for 17 years would have been wiped out in an instant.

- **Be proactive.** Think ahead to what the potential questions may be and answer them before they get asked. Use press releases, FAQ sections, and interviews to stay one step ahead.

Marcus Sheridan, the founder of River Pools and Spas and the best-selling author of *They Ask, You Answer*, has a simple philosophy (summed up in the book's title).[95] If a customer asks a question (within reason), he believes it should be answered. And the customer shouldn't have to work very hard to get that answer. Marcus is a big fan of comprehensive FAQs.

On the River Pools and Spas website, they call it their "Learning Hub," and they answer questions about researching types of pools, what the installation process looks like, how to choose the best pool, and more.

They answer the questions that most businesses would consider taboo. They give advice, on their own website, as to competitive companies that prospective customers might consider during the pool-purchasing process. They even talk about pricing.

I've spoken with Marcus about this. When a prospective customer comes to their website looking for pricing information, River Pools doesn't make them fill out a form to talk to a salesperson. They actually give them the information they need to help figure out, approximately, how much they might be looking at. Because if they don't, the customer is going to be suspicious. The lack of information is going to bring their natural distrust to the surface. By proactively providing transparency they know their customers are going to want, they build trust. And they set themselves apart from the competition.

In doing so, River Pools and Spas has become the 14th ranked pool builder in the United States and is ranked in the top 10 in Community Service, Training, and Websites.[96]

A BALANCING ACT

There's always going to be the balancing act of how much transparency you can give without moving to a Big Brother–esque environment. What works in government will, oftentimes, not fly in the private sector. Just try to get all your employees to walk around with bodycams and see how well that goes over!

While the answer in your company may not be ubiquitous cameras, you can always go back to the ATV model to help guide you:

- **Accountability:** Publicly commit to a goal to which you will be held accountable.

- **T**ransparency: Provide transparency (beyond words) into the process.

- **V**igilance: Increase the vigilance required to deliver on said goal.

Start by publicly committing your goals of accountability through policies or statements. Internally, let it be known that if organizational structure changes are being considered, employees will receive the information available within a certain timeframe. Let them know what to expect. It's hard to run a race with no known finish line. Define it for them so that they can properly pace themselves.

If it's external, make sure all your constituents are aware of your accountability. Tell them how you will ensure that accountability. Invite some of your key constituents in to help ensure that accountability. Have outsiders serve on your board or on advisory councils and allow them the freedom to hold you up to your standards.

Then you must actually provide transparency—in words and actions—to prove that accountability is being adhered to. Communication is the key. Eliminate any doubt by being forthright, honest, and open. Answer the questions you know are likely to exist before they're asked.

If you're doing the first two steps (accountability and transparency) correctly, the vigilance should follow.

THE ATV MODEL IN ACTION

According to the National Partnership for Women & Families,

"overall, women in the United States are paid 82 cents for every dollar paid to men."[97] This is certainly not a new issue, but it's one that some companies are starting to address through accountability and transparency.

Buffer is a software company that helps users manage their social media accounts by scheduling posts and analyzing results. In 2016, Buffer started focusing on equal pay. At that time, they placed a focus on their "unadjusted pay gap," which compares earnings of everyone within their company without taking into consideration their title, experience, or function. According to Hailley Griffis, Head of Public Relations at Buffer, "in the last four years, we've committed to measuring and sharing this gap transparently as we work toward closing it."[98]

Buffer took a public stand on the wage gap, and in doing so, made themselves accountable. To deliver on that accountability, they dedicated themselves to transparency.

How transparent are they? They are about as transparent as you can get. Not only have they publicly stated their problem around wage disparity and publicly committed to working towards parity, but they annually publish their complete analysis and progress. In it, they talk about where they're succeeding and where they still have work to do. They lay out specific areas of focus ("Diversity in our hiring...Transparency...Family Leave").

But that's not all. Buffer goes the extra mile. Since 2013, they've had transparent salaries—they publish every person's salary. Through their website, you can access a spreadsheet that lists every employee *by name*, and shows their role, their location, their level, and their salary. It also shows the 50th percentile comparison salary for someone in that role and level in San Francisco and applies a cost-of-living multiplier based on the individual's location. Elsewhere on their site you can access their salary formula and calculator. It's all there for everyone to see.[99]

It doesn't get any more transparent than that!

Buffer will be the first to admit that, even with that accountability and transparency, they have not yet solved the gender pay-gap problem. They highlight it in their analysis and talk openly about the long-existing systemic issues that have made the problem hard to overcome. But nobody could ever question whether they're working on it!

One positive result beyond the obvious ones of striving for pay parity is that "job applications to work at Buffer significantly increased after the company made its compensation data public."[100]

SumAll is another social media analytics company that has dedicated itself to salary transparency. They have an internal Google Doc that lists every employee's salary, including stock. According to a 2017 interview, then-CEO Dane Atkinson said that the internal transparency "led to annual turnover rates below 10 percent and widespread collaboration between teams."[101]

Zappos, a company we touched on earlier in this book, is also an excellent example of transparency. Transparency is one of their core values. They phrase it as "Build Open and Honest Relationships with Communication." In that vein, they provide their vendors with unprecedented access to the Zappos business, allowing them to see information no other company would normally share. In addition, they provide the same tour of their headquarters I described earlier to anyone who's interested. And remember, these are not cookie-cutter, stop-by-the-gift-shop tours. They take you inside and provide you unfiltered access to see how they operate. They are truly an open book.[102]

PUTTING THE ATV MODEL TO WORK FOR YOU

As we've discussed, the third step in the ATV model is naturally occurring. Once you instill accountability and transparency, the vigilance will follow. Just knowing that your actions are open to evaluation forces you to think more carefully about the paths you take. And that increased awareness itself can lead to the extra vigilance required to avoid complacency.

If you commit to working towards a publicly stated goal and then provide transparency so that everyone can see your progress, you'll naturally be motivated to generate progress. When you don't, you know you'll have to face scrutiny. You'll have to provide explanations. You'll have to admit suboptimal performance. By declaring accountability and providing people the means to hold you to that accountability, vigilance in delivering on your stated goals is the only logical outcome.

To start, work on finding the issues that are most important to both the internal and external constituents to your organization. Of particular interest should be the ones that create the most skepticism and cynicism, the ones that, if left unaddressed, lead to an assumption of wrongdoing or bad intent. Those are the issues that are screaming for accountability.

What are your employees' most frequent complaints or concerns? What do they have the most questions about when provided the opportunity to ask? What prevents them from being happy, and what's most likely to make them leave the organization? What sucks morale and impedes productivity?

What are your customers' most frequent questions? What do they say online, in reviews, and on social media posts? What makes them skeptical of your motives or commitment to their well-being?

These questions are the best places to start in terms of finding issues where you can take accountability and provide transparency.

Think back to the earlier example of River Pools and Spas. While the story was about their transparency, their success starts with their accountability. Their CEO, Marcus Sheridan, has publicly committed his company to his philosophy of "They Ask, You Answer." This commitment requires them to provide transparency. If a customer wants to know about price, River Pools is going to talk price. The accountability and the transparency then promote vigilance. If River Pools avoids a question or refuses to answer, things will get complicated quickly. It's part of who they are. They're committed, and it prevents them from becoming complacent.

If you follow the ATV model of accountability, transparency, and vigilance, you will provide your own extra layer of protection against complacency.

CHAPTER TEN VIGILANCE CHECK

Ask yourself:

1. How much do your customers, consumers, or vendors trust you?

2. How much accountability and transparency are you providing?

3. Where does your company hold power? Over whom do you hold power?

4. Where do you have opportunities to increase accountability and transparency?

CHAPTER ELEVEN

Articulating the Why: Avoiding the Hidden Danger of "Because I Said So"

"Because I said so." It's the ultimate power trip. Admit it. If you're a parent, you've used this one when your kid has asked why they need to do something and why they must do it *now*.

Or maybe you've used it in the workplace when you've gotten push-back from your employees on what you see as simple tasks.

There are several reasons why you might resort to such a tactic. Perhaps you've been down the road many times before and don't feel like explaining it anymore (and are sure that, even if you did, the reasons wouldn't be understood).

Or perhaps you don't really want them to know the reasons (like, "you need to go clean your room again *now* because I'm watching the game and don't want to be bothered").

Or maybe you don't even really know why. Maybe you're asking them to do things that have always been done, and you just don't have good reasons why. For example, your employees ask why they must complete a report every week that never gets used for anything after they complete it, and you're kind of embarrassed because you don't know why that report must be done. And you've never bothered to ask. You just know the report needs to get done, because it's always been done and because *you* had to do it when you were in that role. So, *just shut up and do the report! Because I said so!*

At its core, "Because I said so" is the ultimate in dominance. It's the polar opposite of accountability and transparency. The thinking is, only the powerful and unchecked get to escape rationale.

And, while it may feel good at the time, what it really does is breed complacency because it inhibits critical thinking. If you can't (or won't) explain why you're doing something, you run the risk of doing the wrong thing or doing the right thing in the wrong way.

Now, let's be clear. At times, "because I said so" *must* be enough in the moment. When safety is involved or timing is critical, there may not be time to explain *why*. However, it doesn't mean the why should never come. It may not be practical in the heat of the moment, but never providing the why is usually going to be suboptimal for everyone involved.

Being able to explain your whys is a powerful tool towards vigilance. It forces you to be in the moment, to process stimuli, and to ask questions. It's a close relative to what we covered in the last chapter.

A core part of the vigilance that comes from accountability and transparency is the ability to articulate the why. However, I believe this idea of articulating the why is incredibly important in being able to make the accountability and transparency *believable*. It's a credibility thing.

BEING ABLE TO ARTICULATE THE WHY: LAW ENFORCE-MENT'S ANSWER TO "BECAUSE I SAID SO"

For law enforcement, an officer is given a lot of power from the first day they get that badge. An example of this is the monumental power to take away a citizen's freedom. The power of arrest is enormous. Putting handcuffs on someone, removing them from their home, taking them from their family, and placing them in jail—if there was ever a situation that required the strongest why, this is it. This is especially true since that decision can often lead to even more serious decisions about uses of force (or even deadly force) if the arrest doesn't go as planned, such as if the person resists, fights, runs, or brandishes a weapon. The original why is the starting point in determining if everything else that happened in a chain of events was reasonable.

But there are also lots of other less life-changing powers that are bestowed upon law enforcement officers, such as pulling someone over, stopping someone to have a chat on the street, driving with lights and sirens, going through traffic signals, choosing where we park our cars, etc.

These are all things that come along with the badge. Each one of them has a sliding scale. Each one of them, used incorrectly or at the wrong time, can become criminal. But most of the time, they just come along with the territory.

The key thread that determines whether there are *uses* of power or *abuses* of power is the ability to articulate the why. The ability to articulate *why* we do things (i.e., in a report or on the stand) is what can determine whether a use of power is lawful or not.

The ability to articulate the why is not a nice-to-have. It's a must-have to be a good peace officer. Many of the benefits of articulating the why in a detailed way are on the back end of the decision—being able to write a good report, being a good witness on the stand, communicating with the public—and all of those are important.

But the most important benefit of being able to articulate the why is probably the fact that just knowing you're going to have to do it forces you to consider it beforehand.

COPS ON TV DON'T WRITE REPORTS

Writing reports and doing paperwork in general is a huge part of police work. It's the part rarely seen on TV. In Hollywood, the story line might involve a car chase that ends in a Tactical Vehicle Intervention (TVI, or what you might know by its previous common term, the PIT Maneuver, or Pursuit Intervention Technique). There's a foot bail and chase. The suspect is tackled and arrested. Twenty minutes later, the officers are having a beer at the local bar.

In real life, there could be hours of processing and paperwork after an incident like that, especially these days when many departments have very strict pursuit policies. Questions are going to need to be answered:

- Why was there contact to begin with? Was it a call for service (i.e., someone called in about a vehicle being stolen) or was it self-initiated?

- If it was self-initiated, why? If it was because something looked suspicious, why *exactly* did it look suspicious?

- When the suspect took off, why did you decide to pursue?

Was there immediate perceived danger to yourself or others? What level of crime was suspected? Was it a property crime or a crime against a person? Did you know the identity of the person you were chasing, thereby making it plausible to find them later?

- Why did you make the decision to continue the pursuit instead of cutting it off? Did you have a plan for how you were going to safely bring the pursuit to a conclusion? Were any other units being positioned ahead with stop sticks?

- Why did you perform the TVI maneuver? Why did the dangers of letting the pursuit continue outweigh the dangers of performing the maneuver?

- Why did you use the force level you used when taking the suspect into custody?

- And so on.

Speeds will be examined. Radio traffic will be critiqued. Body camera and in-vehicle camera footage will be reviewed. But it's important to note that the camera footage will likely just show the *what*, not the *why*. The *why* provides the context, the reasoning, and the thought process. Without it, the video is subject to the perceptions and biases of each person who watches it.

As an officer, you should know you will have to answer a lot of whys, and "Because" is not a sufficient answer. Knowing that you're going to be held accountable and will have to be transparent requires you to be prepared and knowledgeable. You need to know the law. You need to know your department's policies and procedures. You need to be able to articulate the whys.

ARTICULATING THE WHY IN BUSINESS

As we've previously discussed, allowing employees to have the discretion and autonomy to make choices that require them to consider the why is incredibly beneficial, not only to their own morale and job satisfaction but to the message they send about your business to your customers.

For example, consider a customer service representative for a credit card company who receives a call from a customer who's been assessed a late fee on a payment. The customer admits that the payment was sent in late but explains that it's the first time they've ever done so. They further explain that they were dealing with an illness in the family and this payment just fell through the cracks. As soon as they realized, they sent in the payment.

Without autonomy, the customer service representative would have no choice. The payment was late. A late charge was assessed. End of story. No thought or reasoning required.

However, with the autonomy and discretion to override such a charge, the representative now must ask themselves why. They can make the choice to waive the fee and can articulate why they did so. If they choose not to reverse the fee, they may end up having to explain why they went that path. "Because I could" is probably not going to be a great answer.

Now let's dial it up.

Abuses of corporate or personal power, while usually not criminal, can lead to severe image and customer satisfaction issues. These, in turn, can open the doors to competition and make it far more likely that your customers will leave in favor of the competition the first chance they get. In extreme cases, as we saw in the previous chapter, they can attract the attention of legislators and start the wheels towards correcting the power paradigm through regulation.

You may develop pricing power or distribution power. Your power might be generated by conquering a category or geography and leaving customers and consumers with few other choices. The power might be generated by contracts and agreements or costs of change if customers want to switch.

Why do you have to pay a new setup fee with your current mobile company every time you purchase a new phone *from them*? Because they said so, that's why. Why do you have to pay an exorbitant change fee with the airline when you want to change your travel but still travel with them? Because they said so, that's why. Why does your agency have to accept slower and more drawn-out payment terms from your extremely large customers? Because they said so, that's why.

Maybe current legislation allows you to make questionable decisions regarding the environment. Perhaps you can get away with it for a while because of your dominance in the industry. When you do get away with it, you may be more likely to make other questionable, yet legal, decisions. But how long until (1) the government steps in, (2) consumers express their concerns in ways that impact your business, or (3) a competitor comes in that provides a better solution?

The more power you've had for longer periods of time, the more likely you are to start abusing it without even realizing it and the more likely your why will be "because I said so."

THE WHYS INSIDE YOUR ORGANIZATION

Being able to articulate the why is also incredibly important to the internal workings of an organization. Just like in law enforcement, the inability to articulate the why within an organization can lead to an erosion of trust and a lack of confidence in decision-making.

While it may be strangely satisfying for a boss to tell their employees "because I said so," those employees will likely walk away dissatisfied and distrustful. They will make assumptions about the reasons that range from their being evil in nature to being not credible at all. Therefore, the resulting impressions will range from those of villainy to those of incompetence. None of these is good or fosters productive, trusting work environments.

The sheer act of articulating the why, though, demonstrates that the why was considered. It shows a desire for fairness, for competence, and for transparency, all of which foster trust and productivity.

PATAGONIA'S DEEPER WHYS

Understanding your why can also be very powerful when it goes deeper into the true purpose and reason-to-be for the company. Organizations that can articulate the overall why of what they do have the ability to connect with consumers, customers, vendors, and employees in the most meaningful ways. Additionally, really understanding your true why helps to guide all the other why questions along the way.

Take, for example, the outdoor clothing retailer Patagonia. When you search them on Google, the snippet description they provide of themselves is:

> *Patagonia is a designer of outdoor clothing and gear*
> *for the silent sports: climbing, surfing, skiing and*
> *snowboarding, fly fishing, and trail running.*[103]

That description, in and of itself, is pretty satisfying. When deciding whether to pursue a certain product line, it's easy for someone to describe the why. If it's a basketball jersey, it's probably going to be a no. If it's a fly-fishing hat, it's more likely a go.

But Patagonia is much more than clothing for the "silent sports." When you get to the website, there are four major menu items listed:

- Shop

- Activism

- Sports

- Stories

Of course, "Shop" makes sense when visiting a clothing online store. But "Activism?"

Click that link and you get to a page that has a background video of people protesting. The headline of the page is:

> *We're in business to save our home planet. We aim to use*
> *the resources we have—our voice, our business and our*
> *community—to do something about our climate crisis.*

Pretty powerful stuff. They're stating publicly that they're not in the business of selling clothes. They're in the business of saving the planet!

As you scroll down the page, there's more:

We're Part of a Movement for Change. From supporting youth fighting against oil drilling to suing the president, we take action on the most pressing environmental issues facing our world.

They go on to outline activism stories they're involved in. They describe the 1 percent Earth Tax they impose on themselves. They put 1 percent from everything back into the planet by supporting environmental nonprofits. They highlight employees who are deemed "Global Sport Activists" and "are using their roles in the sport community to drive positive social and environmental change."

Elsewhere on their site they provide a scathing condemnation of the clothing industry. They point out how the "clothing industry contributes 10 percent of the pollution driving the climate crisis" and they call out "Big Fashion" saying "the world's largest clothing brands hid dirty and irresponsible practices and misuse words like 'sustainable,' 'green,' and 'conscious.'"

And then Patagonia takes a stand. They say, "Together, we can change how clothes are made," and they commit to recycling and to lower emissions, stating that "72 percent of our materials are made from recycled fibers." They grow all their own cotton organically. They're "changing how we grow food and fiber." They take care of their employees. They recommend the reuse of clothing—not what you would expect from a company that *sells new clothing*.

While many others talk the talk regarding corporate responsibility, Patagonia walks the walk. They state their intentions publicly so they can be held accountable. And they provide the transparency to allow others to hold them accountable.

You can imagine, then, with this much work put into the why of the company, individual decisions are not that difficult to explain. The public documentation of what they believe in and what their business is provides a roadmap to employees. It's their equivalent of policies and procedures. Being knowledgeable of them provides the ability to articulate the why of anything. Why they sell a certain item. Why they source their raw materials from one place versus another. Why they choose to get involved in a cause. Why they're connected to their customers, their vendors, their employees.

WHAT IS YOUR PURPOSE?

You're probably familiar with vision, mission, and values statements. They're a staple for most businesses, and in many cases, a lot of time and energy is spent getting the words just right so that they say so much that they barely say anything useful at all.

Even Disney has figured out a way to muck it up. Ask most people what Disney's mission or vision is (most people don't really know the difference), and they'll eagerly answer something along the lines of, "To make people happy." This sounds fantastic (albeit broad)— except it's not true, at least not anymore. At the start, that's perhaps how Walt Disney articulated his why, but if you go to the Disney website now, here's what you'll find:

> *The mission of The Walt Disney Company is to entertain, inform, and inspire people around the globe through the power of unparalleled storytelling, reflecting the iconic brands, creative minds, and innovative technologies that make ours the world's premier entertainment company.*[104]

Not quite as pithy, eh?

Historically, your vision is supposed to represent your organization's aspirations, what it hopes to achieve in the future, what it's working towards. The mission, then, describes what the organization needs to do now to best achieve that vision. The values statement then lays out how people within the organization are expected to behave in the execution of the mission in the pursuit of the vision.

Often, companies confuse the vision and mission statements. Or maybe they just do one statement that covers them both. They tend to focus on what the company does and how it strives to do it. Most often, these tend to be *internally* focused.

More useful in being able to articulate the why, though, would be a purpose statement, a declaration of *why* the company even exists in the first place. For example, consider the food company Kellogg's. On their website they lay out just two statements:

Our Vision: A good and just world where people are not just fed but fulfilled.

Our Purpose: Creating better days and a place at the table for everyone through our trusted food brands.[105]

Southwest Airlines lays out their promises and their values, but also focuses on just two statements (leaving out a mission statement):[106]

Vision: To be the world's most loved, most efficient, and most profitable airline.

*Purpose: Connect People to what's important in their lives
through friendly, reliable, and low-cost air travel.*

Even by the style of how they write that purpose, they're communicating their hierarchy of why. By capitalizing "People" they made it clear what drives them—and what should drive every decision.

Financial services firm Charles Schwab doesn't mince words on their website. They don't label their different statements. They just lead with their purpose:

*Charles Schwab exists to help people achieve
better financial outcomes.*

Think about how your organization, after a ton of meetings, would write that statement. Would it be so clear and outward focused? Or would it grow in length with every discussion until it is so all-encompassing that it essentially says nothing?

As you can see, when done correctly, a purpose statement can help provide the why. By laying bare the reason the company even exists (beyond just making money), it provides a roadmap for understanding why it does the things it does. And why it doesn't do the things it doesn't do.

If you don't have a purpose statement, now would be a good time to start on one. If the organization can't define its ultimate why, how can the individuals within it articulate their own?

FORCE YOURSELF TO ASK
WHY BEFORE SOMEONE ELSE DOES

Beyond not having a purpose statement, you can also watch out for these telltale signs that indicate you aren't able or willing to articulate the why:

- making decisions because *you can* without reasons that go beyond your own benefit

- inability of employees to withstand scrutiny on their decisions

- disgruntled or dissatisfied customers, consumers, employees, family members, or other constituents

- internal or external confusion around your company

- poorly designed or missing policies and procedures

- a general lack of trust or an assumption that you're up to no good

- the appearance of competitors who are clearly defining their whys, sometimes directly against you

- government interest in your business/industry/category

- a feeling of entitlement or invincibility

- a lack of concern for the ecosystem or environment in which you reside/compete/interact

- a reliance on legislation to explain why you're allowed to do what you do

- a lack of loyalty from current customers, consumers, or employees

- a change in the types of things you do now that you have power, in comparison with when you did not

- a feeling that, based on history, you've somehow earned the right to act the way you do, without explanation

Take an honest look at the points above. If some (or all) of these ring true, you're likely lacking in being able to articulate the why. This may mean that you're abusing the power you've accumulated without even realizing it. Or maybe you're abusing your power, avoiding the whys, and you already did know it, which is worse.

If either of these is true, you need to address it now before someone else addresses it for you. Rest assured, sooner or later, the pendulum will swing. Whether it involves government intervention, a competitive attack, or just your kids growing up and no longer fearing you, the power that allows you to say "because I said so" rarely lasts forever.

Here are some things you can start doing right away to create an environment more conducive to articulating the whys:

- **Clearly, and publicly, define your overall whys**. As discussed above, the best place to start may be with a purpose statement. At the very least, document your policies and procedures to provide a common roadmap to the whys and ensure everyone in your organization (or family) is knowledgeable about it and on board. Be committed and unwavering.

- **Commit yourself to providing answers to the whys** and ensure there's an understanding that everyone else in the organization will be expected to do so as well.

- **Encourage the asking of why—incessantly, like a child**. It usually only becomes *really* annoying when you've reached the point where you don't know the answer. When that happens, find it out.

- **Avoid, whenever possible, "Because I said so."** As I stated at the start of this chapter, though, sometimes that must be enough, especially in times that threaten safety. You don't want to have to explain why someone needs to get out of a burning house while it's on fire. But you should loop back as soon as the danger has passed and discuss the why. If, for nothing else, it lets the person know there was a well thought-out why, which fosters learning and trust.

Just by doing the above, you'll increase your vigilance and create your own natural barriers to complacency.

CHAPTER ELEVEN VIGILANCE CHECK

Ask yourself:

1. Have you ever answered a question with, "Because I said so"? Why?

2. How good are you, your team, or your organization at articulating the whys of what you do?

3. Does your organization have a purpose statement?

4. If not, what is the purpose of your organization?

5. What might you start doing by better understanding this purpose? What might you stop doing?

CHAPTER TWELVE

Metrics Gone Wrong: No Blood Doesn't Mean No Bleeding

I was on patrol one summer day when a call came out about a mountain biker who was down on a back-country bike trail. It wasn't the easiest spot to get to with a police SUV, but several of us got there quickly. Once there, we immediately oriented ourselves to the situation.

The biker was relatively young (probably in his 40s) and looked athletic. There was no helmet on his head, but one was found nearby. I don't know much about bikes, but his looked pretty capable. It looked like he was probably thrown over the handlebars when he crashed.

He was able to talk but he wasn't making any sense. Words were coming out, but no coherent sentences. It quickly devolved into more of a mumble. The volume and cadence of his attempted speech, though, told us he was in pain and upset. We didn't see any blood or open wounds. There weren't any obvious fractures or displacements.

He was lying on his back. One deputy stabilized his head and neck to prevent any further damage. The goal was to keep him still until medical help could arrive.

As we waited for EMS, we didn't know exactly what was wrong with him. But experience told us that his confusion and difficulty speaking or understanding speech, combined with the type of accident and the fact that the helmet had been thrown from his head, could be signs that there was some type of internal injury from the accident.

In the minutes before medical personnel arrived, and while we tried to keep the man looking and talking to us, he began to calm, was talking less, and suddenly stopped breathing.

Deputies immediately started compressions. EMTs arrived shortly afterwards and were able to get an automated chest compression machine going along with mechanical breathing assistance. They transported him back on the trail using an all-terrain vehicle to a waiting helicopter that flew him to the hospital; they suspected a brain bleed.

Two things that I already knew were hammered home by that incident:

1. Life is precious and fleeting. We can do everything right and things can still go horribly wrong. Don't ever take it for granted.

2. Just because you don't see blood, that doesn't mean there isn't bleeding.

METRICS CAN BE ENLIGHTENING OR DECEIVING

As you strive towards the vigilance that accountability and transparency can provide, you'll likely look towards metrics to help gauge and communicate your performance and highlight areas that require more attention.

Just so we have a common understanding, when I refer to *metrics* here, I mean quantitative measurements that are used for recording, tracking, and comparing performance. Metrics can be incredibly helpful in determining success versus failure, developing early warning signals when things are off, comparing past and current performance and understanding the differences, and much more.

However, metrics are only useful if they're the right metrics, they're actionable, they're interpreted correctly, and they're not abused. When metrics are used incorrectly or even abused, a false sense of security can be the result. That false sense of security can push you towards the opposite result of the desired vigilance—complacency.

THE DANGER OF FAULTY METRICS IN MEDICAL TRAUMAS

As deputies, we train a lot in trauma first aid. This mostly involves correctly stabilizing people who may have neck or back injuries, reversing the effects of opioid overdoses, providing electronic defibrillation and/or CPR to people having a cardiac event, and trying to manage traumatic bleeding wounds that result from accidents, gunshots, or stabbings.

The metrics we use and the tools we have at our disposal are limited. Even though we're often the first on scene for medical events, we're law enforcement and not doctors. Most of our response can be boiled down to simple if/thens.

If someone suffers a fall or a traumatic accident and there's any doubt, then we stabilize the head and neck until medical personnel can apply a brace.

If the information we have suggests that a subject has overdosed on opioids, then we apply NARCAN (if we have it), and if they're breathing, we get them into the recovery position.

If someone isn't breathing or has no pulse, then we start compressions immediately.

And if someone has an obvious wound that is generating a large amount of blood or pulsating bleeding, then we apply tourniquets (some wounds may need more than one), hemostatic gauze, and pressure bandages. If the wound is in the chest, we use chest seals.

Of course, if none of the above applies, it doesn't mean there isn't anything wrong with the patient. It just means it's probably beyond our capabilities to help past keeping them calm, still, and as comfortable as possible until the medical crew arrives (which is usually very quickly in our county).

We understand the limitations of the metrics we can apply in these types of situations. We know what to do when there's visible bleeding. But we also know that just because there isn't visible bleeding, it doesn't mean all is well. Care and urgency are still required. Even in situations where there's been a fall or an accident and all indications would be that the person is fine, we still recommend they undergo some level of medical evaluation, even if that means just getting a quick once-over by an EMT.

People are often reluctant. They feel fine, they say. They have no broken bones or cuts, just a slight headache. They resist medical attention. Those people are potentially working off the wrong metrics. And the consequences could be catastrophic.

On March 16, 2009, English actress Natasha Richardson (the wife of actor Liam Neeson) fell on a beginner's trail while taking a ski lesson at the Mont Tremblant ski resort in Quebec, Canada. She wasn't wearing a helmet but also didn't collide with anything when she fell. At first, she felt and looked fine and even was reported to have joked about the fall. As part of their protocol, the ski patrol at Mont Tremblant responded to the scene. She was transported by sleigh to the infirmary. While there, she felt fine and signed herself out. She walked back to her hotel along with her ski instructor. About an hour and a half later, Ms. Richardson began feeling ill and an ambulance was sent. She was taken to one hospital and then transferred to another before she was flown to a third hospital in New York City, where she died on March 18 from bleeding between her skull and her brain.[107]

Ms. Richardson initially felt fine and looked fine. She hadn't collided with anything. And yet those metrics didn't reveal the underlying condition. Just because you don't see blood doesn't mean there isn't bleeding.

The implications of this concept to both your professional and personal life are both broad and important. Metrics used incorrectly can be just as damaging and dangerous as not using metrics at all.

Maybe you've historically used a metric that tracks the number of customer complaints you receive. You notice the numbers are going down and you feel good about that. But what if it's just because your customers don't care enough to complain to you anymore? What if they've taken their complaints to other places instead of communicating them directly to you? If you aren't adapting with the times and truly understanding whether your metric is telling you something real, then it can lead you to a false sense of security. A level of overconfidence. Complacency.

To reiterate what I said at the start of this chapter, there are two ways that metrics can end up doing more harm than good:

- using metrics incorrectly
- allowing the metrics to be abused or gamed

USING METRICS INCORRECTLY

Eric Reis is an entrepreneur, a blogger, and the author of *The Lean Startup*. Eric uses the term vanity metrics to describe "numbers that look good on paper but aren't action-oriented: website hits, message volume, or 'billions and billions served.' They look great in a press release, but what do they accomplish?"

Mr. Reis also talks about what's become a widely used explanation of what makes good metrics. Specifically, they need to be "actionable, accessible, and auditable." By this, he means that the metrics you use must provide data you can act on, they must be easily accessed by people across the organization, and they must be based on data that can be checked.[108]

Vanity metrics are dangerous, because they can make us feel good, safe, and successful when they may not actually mean anything. They're worse than not being vigilant, because they make us believe we *are* being vigilant when that vigilance is actually misguided. They breed complacency. Take, for example, web page views.

Throughout the year, as ManageCamp Inc. prepares for our annual Brand ManageCamp, we communicate with our audience (and potential audience) through various means, including direct mail, email, social media, search engines, and more. As you might imagine, each time we distribute a communication, we're eager to see how successful it was. Early in our history, we would rely on web page views as an easy way for us to gauge success. The more page views, the more people had visited the site. This had to be good, right?

Well, the answer was not as simple as the metric would have us believe. Over time, we began to realize that page views weren't translating to what we were really interested in, which were conference registrations.

This was happening for several reasons. Our email distribution service was recording a massive number of opens that would result in website page hits that turned out to be somewhat less than real. One reason involved the way corporate email servers were testing our site to see if it was spam or not, resulting in what looked like page views but really weren't. Another reason involved the way images in the emails were used (stored on our website versus in a cloud server elsewhere).

If you know a lot about this kind of stuff, you may be shaking your head right now. Let's suffice it to say that we weren't very sophisticated (it was basically myself and my wife running the business, and neither of us knew much about the technical side of websites and email marketing).

Nonetheless, we'd send an email, and we'd get super excited. Look at that traffic! But the registrations for the conference wouldn't follow. Separately, we'd send out an email only to past attendees. The website hits would be far lower, but the registrations would pour in.

Obviously, we had a problem. Website hits and page views were easy to measure. They were accessible (anybody in our organization could see them). They were even auditable to a certain extent (we could go back and verify the numbers on our website dashboard).

But they weren't actionable. First off, they weren't measurements that actually translated to our area of most interest. They didn't translate to sales, customer satisfaction, loyalty, or really anything that meant something beyond our egos.

Secondly, they weren't predictive. High page views didn't accurately predict any of the things mentioned above that we actually cared about. They didn't predict conference registrations. The problem was our conference was once a year. For a large part of the year, we didn't expect registrations at all.

Finally, we came to realize, these metrics weren't even real. The numbers were artificially inflated due to technical issues and weren't even telling us what we thought they were telling us.

By focusing on this metric (that was easy to see) and not others that required more digging (like time spent on a page, conversion from pages, number of pages viewed each visit, number of repeat visits, etc.), we were missing the equivalent of the internal bleeding. We thought our content was providing healthy interaction when it was not, and that created a false sense of confidence and security. If we had sat back on that false sense of confidence telling us to just keep doing what we were doing, by the time we figured out the registrations weren't coming, it would have been too late.

Once we had an inkling that something was wrong, we started to pay more attention to numbers of pages viewed, time spent per page, and various conversion metrics that showed how sticky and persuasive our site was to the people who visited it. We also spent more time looking at points of origins for visitors to see which vehicles were delivering the highest valued prospects. And we were able to get a way more accurate view of successful content versus poorly performing content so that we could make the real-time adjustments we needed to survive.

What vanity metrics are you using today? Are you using metrics that make you feel good, but may not really be telling you anything meaningful? Are you using metrics that are easy, that are visible, and that are auditable, but that, nonetheless, don't tell you anything actionable?

In the case of vanity metrics, the issue may be that you're using the wrong metrics or, in some cases, not enough metrics. However, a similar problem can occur if you are using *too many* metrics.

MORE IS NOT NECESSARILY BETTER

Sometimes we try to make up for our fear of inaccuracy by adding more metrics to the mix, even if they're not necessarily the right ones.

This phenomenon was laid out brilliantly by Malcolm Gladwell in his best-selling book *Blink*.[109] In it, he discusses the story of Chicago's Cook County Hospital in the late 1990s. The Emergency Department was wasting a lot of money and resources due to their inability to correctly determine if patients presenting with chest pains were experiencing a heart attack or not.

Doctors were making decisions based on gathering a large amount of information, including visual cues they picked up from patients regarding age, physical health, weight, etc. But different doctors were making different decisions when presented with the *same* information. And, often, they were wrong.

Because they knew they might be wrong, they overcompensated by erring on the side of diagnosing a heart attack, just to be safe. Their version of complacency meant that the doctors felt they could rest easier knowing that they were likely not missing most actual heart attacks. But the unseen danger was in the overcrowding and financial inefficiency it created, putting a strain on the Emergency Department and the entire hospital community.

To increase diagnosis accuracy and efficiency to ultimately provide a better level of service and save money, they turned to the work of a cardiologist named Lee Goldman, who had developed a decision tree for treating patients with chest pain that relied on only four metrics:

- the patient's ECG reading

- whether or not the pain felt by the patient was unstable angina

- whether or not there was fluid detected in the patient's lungs

- whether or not the patient's systolic blood pressure was under 100

None of these metrics required even seeing the patient. They didn't consider the age, weight, skin color, or physical appearance of the patient. They didn't even consider whether the patient was diabetic or a smoker or anything else, just those four metrics. A decision tree was used based on different combinations of answers from those four metrics that would tell the doctors exactly what to do.

When doctors could use any information they wanted (including skin color, gender, age, etc.), they were right between 75 to 89 percent of the time. Those using the algorithm were right more than 95 percent of the time.

Less information was actually more.

By focusing on the wrong metrics, you can get a false sense of security. You can fail to see or recognize dangers before they become a problem. You can have the double whammy of thinking you're being vigilant when, in reality, you aren't. Or you could be clouding the whole situation, making it harder and harder to trust your decisions.

Spend the time to find the absolute minimum number of the right metrics that can be actionable, accessible, and auditable.

METRICS ABUSE (THE COBRA EFFECT)

Consider the following two laws as they relate to creating measurements for the purpose of making decisions:

Donald T. Campbell was a psychologist and social scientist. Campbell's Law states:

> The more any quantitative social indicator is used for social decision-making, the more subject it will be to corruption pressures and the more apt it will be to distort and corrupt the social processes it is intended to monitor.[110]

Goodhart's Law (written by anthropologist Marily Strathern as a generalization of the work of British economist Charles Goodhart) says:

> When a measure becomes a target, it ceases to be a good measure.[111]

Both laws are meant to point out the inevitable draw of abusing or gaming metrics and the propensity for people to anticipate the effects of the metrics and then take actions to alter the outcome, especially when the metrics are being used to measure someone's performance or determine compensation models.

A classic example is if a police department evaluates officers based on the number of tickets written. What could go wrong there? Well, cops might try to write as many tickets as possible, to the detriment of other activities (and public perception). What if it were the reverse and officers were rewarded for writing fewer tickets? You can almost bet traffic accidents and traffic fatalities would rise as people began to realize they could drive it like they stole it.

Another area where metrics can potentially be gamed in law enforcement is in the measurement of categories of crimes. Let's say there was pressure to lower the number of reported violent crimes. But who classifies calls? Initially, they're classified by Dispatch based on the information from the caller. The officer or supervisor can then change the call type based on what they find out. There's a lot of discretion in there. If there was a perceived incentive to classify calls as nonviolent, for example, an assault or a domestic violence call could be reclassified as a disturbance or a citizen's assist. Would it help the metric? Sure. Would it also raise other issues in terms of providing a distorted view of reality that could lead to bad (i.e., overconfident) decisions on funding and staffing? Absolutely.

Let's look at some non-police examples. Consider airline on-time performance. A flight is generally considered to be on time for reporting purposes if it arrives within 15 minutes of its scheduled arrival time. You might even be the type of person who chooses their flights by looking at the on-time percentages.

Who determines the scheduled arrival time (or, really, the flight duration time)? The airlines, of course. So, you can easily see the problem. Which one is the airline encouraged to do by this metric: reflect flight time as accurately as possible, or build in buffers to allow for a higher on-time percentage? The latter, obviously.

I often fly between Denver and Las Vegas. According to Travelmath. com, the actual in-air time for the flight from Denver to Las Vegas is 1 hour and 27 minutes. The total time from gate to gate is 1 hour and 46 minutes.[112]

But United lists a direct flight at 1 hour and 59 minutes (United Flight 484, departing at 3:50 p.m. on Friday, April 23, 2021), a buffer of 13 minutes.

Take that buffer of 13 minutes they've built in and combine it with the 15-minute buffer already used to determine a flight's on-time status. That gives them the potential to be 28 minutes later than the actual flight duration would suggest and still get to say they're on time.

So, while on-time performance might look like a usable metric to evaluate an airline's customer experience, you can see that it's too easily gamed, compromising its usefulness. Depending on how much cushion each airline uses, you can have several airlines that experience the same flight times but show drastically different on-time performance.

Nearly every institution can be affected negatively by metrics gone bad. Take, for example, the American education system and the practice of teaching to the test. The No Child Left Behind Act of 2002 supported standards-based education reform that resulted in setting standards and measurable goals to improve educational outcomes.[113] It requires states, in order to receive federal school funding, to use standardized tests to show progress.

Performance by schools on standardized tests affects rankings, evaluations, and funding. This, in turn, results in a great deal of pressure being placed on districts, schools, and, ultimately, teachers to ensure their students do well on the standardized tests.

The result, teaching to the test, involves teachers focusing their curriculum on the narrow range of skills of knowledge that will be tested, as opposed to the broader understanding of the subject matter. In the end, higher test scores may be achieved, but potentially at the risk of the overall learning success of the students and the passion the teachers have for their jobs.

Sometimes it goes beyond teaching to the test and wanders into the realm of corruption. Much has been written about how the No Child Left Behind Act encouraged corruption and cheating. Consider this from 2006, written by W. James Popham (professor emeritus at UCLA's Graduate School of Education and Information Studies):

> *An astonishing amount of cheating is taking place on the tests that measure progress under the federal No Child Left Behind Act. And the cheating I'm referring to isn't coming from the kids.*

> *It's rare for a week to go by lately without encountering one or more news reports describing how educators have been caught cheating on their states' federally mandated tests. Much of this reported cheating stems from the actions of school or district administrators. But a number of classroom teachers have also been identified as benders and breakers of the No Child Left Behind tests' rules.*[114]

There's a name for when you try to fix a problem but end up creating a whole new problem. It's called the Cobra Effect, and it originates from when the British ruled colonial India. At the time, there was concern over the number of venomous cobras in Delhi. A bounty was offered for every dead cobra. So, what did the enterprising people of Delhi do? They began breeding cobras to kill and collect the bounty, of course. The government became aware and put a stop to the program, resulting in all the bred cobras to be released. In the end, there were far more venomous cobras to deal with than before the bounty.[115]

When implementing metrics, you must consider the unintended consequences you could be bringing about by those whose performance is measured by them. When people or organizations game a metric, the metric no longer delivers actionable information. At best, it becomes useless. At worst, it encourages the overconfidence that can result in complacency.

USING METRICS TO PROMOTE VIGILANCE, NOT UNDERMINE IT

Whenever I think of metrics, I think of the guy on the bike, and I think of Natasha Richardson. I remember that just because there's no blood, it doesn't mean there isn't any bleeding.

I consider the fact that metrics can go wrong if they're (1) measuring the wrong things or (2) encouraging cheating.

And then I think about the four ways we can use the *right* metrics the *right* way—ensuring they promote vigilance as opposed to undermining it and that they provide us with the information we need to make informed and accurate decisions:

- **Find the metrics that measure the things that matter.** These are the ones that correlate to success. Not the vanity measures (like page views) or the ones that are easiest to measure, but the ones that truly can be directly tied to desired outcomes. Remember that *more* is not necessarily *bet-*

ter when it comes to metrics. If done correctly, this should take some time and should reflect a deep understanding of your purpose, your key goals, and objectives. What do you want to make sure is managed?

- **Make sure the metrics are actionable, accessible, and auditable.** People need to be able to trust and understand the metrics. Everyone who needs to know about them needs to be able to easily see them. The metrics need to be verifiable and hold up to scrutiny. And they must provide information that you can *act* on.

- **Look for correlation versus causation.** Understand the difference between the two and put in the work to understand which applies to your metric. Whether one outcome is caused by another or just correlated to it, the information can be very useful. But a lack of understanding of which it is (caused or correlated) can lead to the wrong decisions.

- **Don't get gamed**. Or, more accurately, don't encourage gaming. Beware of the Cobra Effect and its unintended consequences. Think through the potential implications of your metrics and what you're encouraging people to do. If there is a way your metric can be perverted, it probably will be perverted, especially if it's directly tied to performance appraisals or compensation. Anticipate the potential abuse, and devise countermeasures to help prevent them. Alternatively, if you find yourself working hard to stem the cheating that the metric has brought on, really question why you're using that metric in the first place.

The right metrics, used the right way, can be invaluable in helping you gauge performance and raise awareness of potential threats long before they become major problems. This awareness of the dangers around you and the maintenance of an early warning system will help you combat the overconfidence, smugness, and false sense of security that can lead to complacency.

CHAPTER TWELVE VIGILANCE CHECK

Ask yourself:

1. What vanity metrics are you currently using?

2. What metrics are you using incorrectly?

3. What metrics are you using that could be eliminated?

4. What metrics are currently being gamed?

5. Are your metrics actionable, accessible, and auditable?

CHAPTER THIRTEEN

―――――

Be Vigilant! Always

"Not me. Never."

It's what we thought in the police academy when we scrutinized videos of calls that had gone very wrong.

It's what you've thought when hearing about companies that had once been big, powerful, and successful, but ended in bankruptcy—failures that seemed so avoidable that they might have even made you angry. How could they have been so blind?

The hope in writing this book has been to help you realize that *they* could very easily be *us*, that we're all susceptible to the overconfidence and self-satisfaction that can lead to complacency.

And complacency kills.

In law enforcement, it can quite literally do so. But it's no less deadly for businesses, careers, and relationships.

Complacency is like a virus that never really goes away. It's always there, in the background, just waiting for the right conditions for it to thrive.

The irony is that the more successful we are, the riper the conditions for it to take hold. It can be silent and subtle and, without understanding it, can take hold without your even realizing.

Complacency is a word we're all familiar with. We hear it and see it all the time. Journalists, sports broadcasters, politicians, and businesspeople use it without giving it a second thought.

The word complacency is often thrown out there as a warning, as something to avoid. But it's rarely explained. Even rarer still is when anyone follows that warning with any real advice on how to avoid it.

This book has been about helping you build a deeper understanding of complacency—why it develops, where it comes from, and how to recognize it.

More importantly, this book has been about giving you that advice—the tools, techniques, and processes—you need to avoid it. To open your eyes and raise your awareness level. To let you recognize the warning signs and implement changes that will make a real difference. To position you to conquer complacency.

The lessons I've covered were born from my late-in-life journey into law enforcement. They are things I see us doing every day to help fight back the complacency that can come with a job where most everything goes right—but when it goes wrong, it goes *very* wrong.

Complacency makes us vulnerable. And competition loves vulnerability. It invites trouble.

As I was planning this final chapter, I was also watching some English football. It was Chelsea versus Tottenham, and it was just over

26 minutes into the game. A player from Chelsea had made a lazy pass and Tottenham had taken advantage, nearly scoring a goal.

One of the commentators, English ex–professional footballer Graeme Le Saux, described what had happened in this way:

> *Chelsea getting a little bit complacent with the final pass, Zouma there hitting a ball that was never going to reach its target, and Tottenham using that as a signal to break.*

Mr. Le Saux summed up the core danger of complacency in that one description. Complacency signals vulnerability. It shows weakness. It invites attack.

While reading this book, you've likely thought about your own areas in business and in life where you've become complacent, signaling vulnerability and weakness, inviting competition to attack. That's great!

The trick is to do something about that complacency, to stop it in its tracks, to push it back, and make it less likely to happen again.

And that's why this book hasn't been about the doom and gloom of complacency. It's been about the positive impact we can bring by understanding complacency and leveraging simple tools of vigilance to raise our awareness and beat it back.

This journey into understanding complacency and how intentional vigilance can help combat it has had a profound effect on my own business.

Over the many years since 2003 that I've been running the annual Brand ManageCamp marketing conference, we've experienced consistent (if not moderate) success. What we didn't realize over those years, though, was that we were slowly becoming complacent. And it was setting us up for a very difficult time.

When I started Brand ManageCamp, I was full of vim and vigor and was passionate about the deficiencies I saw in the marketing conference industry. It was clear where the competition was missing the mark, where they were vulnerable, where they had become complacent. They were heavy on talk and light on action. They delivered more sales pitches than actionable insights. They dropped the ball on the overall experience—not sticking to agenda timing, delivering less-than-optimal audio/visual executions, and skimping on the food and beverage. They had developed a reliance on sponsorship and on panel discussions to pad their attendee list (at the detriment of the experience for their actual paying attendees).

Over and over, I saw attendees at these established conferences leave early, only to come back the next year having seemingly forgotten the previous year's disappointment. The bar was low. So, we crafted the event that improved on all these elements. And people came.

Our success, though, dulled our senses. We experienced survivorship bias (Chapter Two). Obviously, what we were doing was working. And it was easy to keep doing what we were doing. Why change what isn't broken?

As the years rolled on, we missed some key developments in the marketplace. Changes in technology. Changes in how our target market consumed information. Changes in budgets and attitudes on travel and training. These changes were slow and gradual, but they were happening. And they presented threats to our way of doing business (Chapter Three). We had an inkling that these changes would affect our business at some time in the future, but the changes to our industry were slow. We felt we probably had time.

From the start, Brand ManageCamp was a live conference. We moved it around the country for several years before finding a home in Las Vegas. There we found the perfect combination of meeting space, cost, and accessibility.

We were so comfortable doing live events in Las Vegas that we began to lag far behind in the trend of virtual events and content. We didn't develop any expertise in livestreaming. We used video, but not to its full potential.

We were, essentially, standing on the X (Chapter Four). Our predictability was appreciated by our loyal attendees who knew they were always going to get the quality event they had come to know and love. The speakers and the topics would change, but everything about the execution would remain the same. They knew they would walk away with tons of actionable insights, tools, and techniques they could use right away to build stronger customer and consumer relationships; build, manage, and grow more profitable brands; and become better leaders. They also knew they were not going to be sold to by a barrage of vendors.

At the end of each successful conference, we would pat ourselves on the back: another year of satisfied attendees (our satisfaction scores were in the 97 percent range). We only conducted debriefings to address things that had gone noticeably wrong. We never talked about how we could continue to improve on what was going well. Some of this was due to a fear of messing with success. Some of this was, if I'm being honest, laziness (Chapter Five).

The cost of our predictability was the fact that we didn't evolve. By essentially keeping one eye closed and being laser-focused on delivering the best live conference experience, we missed what was going on in the periphery—the rise of virtual and livestreaming (Chapter Six).

Over the years, I'd become very confident in my understanding of our target market and how to deliver the best live conference experience to them. I was so confident that I knew the best way, that those on my team would be nervous to bring up new ideas. They were certain that if things weren't done my way, I'd redo them myself. They weren't wrong. There was no autonomy, just prescribed execution of my plans (Chapter Eight).

With all these factors in play, it's no surprise that complacency had settled in. All the conditions made it easy for it to take hold, to make us vulnerable, and to put us at risk. It hadn't happened overnight. It had taken years. It had snuck in, under the radar, and become imbedded in the way we did things.

There's no doubt that the COVID-19 pandemic sped up what was already inevitable, but the reality of what we had missed came quickly. In February 2020, we were heavily into the normal start of our marketing campaign for our 18th annual Brand ManageCamp event to be held in Las Vegas in September. A few weeks later, live events were seemingly a thing of the past.

It quickly became clear that we'd have to pivot, that we'd need to move our conference into the virtual realm. It also quickly became clear that we were woefully unprepared to do so.

Not only were our technical skills in livestreaming lacking, but we were also strategically unprepared for what a move to virtual would do to the world of conferences and training events. Overnight, everything changed, not the least of which was the value proposition in the mind of the attendee. With the incredible influx of free content, the willingness to pay for content diminished greatly. We hadn't really considered this scenario.

We found ourselves in what felt like the same position we were in 18 years earlier when we were first starting out. We had to re-find our place in the market and begin building our reputation once again.

When this happened, I was already in the midst of writing this book. I already knew what complacency was and how dangerous it was. I was already able to apply the principles to my own business.

But, until the pandemic hit, I was unaware of how much danger my business was truly in. Even while writing a book on complacency, I failed to recognize the depths of my own overconfidence, and I learned firsthand the perils that presented.

This story has a happy ending, though (at least for now). We were able to make our pivot extremely quickly. We adapted our business model and our offerings to the new reality. We became proficient in livestreaming and in understanding how people learn in the virtual environment. People signed up. And we delivered our 18th annual Brand ManageCamp virtually, with no technical glitches and the same attendee satisfaction scores we had enjoyed in our live events.

And now we look forward with a newfound vigilance. Using the lessons that I've learned from my late-in-life venture into law enforcement, we're forging a new future for our conference.

We now recognize the effect of survivorship bias and overconfidence on our business. We're creating procedures and responsibilities aimed at early identification of threats. We're conscious of the importance of strategic unpredictability, and we actively consider how to get off the X. We brief and debrief regularly, even when things are going right. We practice keeping both eyes open and seeing beyond our perceived target. We're constantly on the lookout for places that we can create good habits and eliminate (or change) bad ones. We've also identified some key areas where we could benefit from increased accountability and transparency. We're constantly making sure we can articulate our whys. We're also reevaluating the measurements we use to keep track of our wins and losses, always making sure they are promoting vigilance and not suppressing it. And, throughout this entire process, I've learned to let go and have enjoyed the fruits of the team's newfound autonomy and engagement.

I truly hope that this book has been as valuable for you as it's been for me. Not only am I incorporating elements from each chapter into my business, but I also use them every day in my personal life, helping to strengthen my relationships and avoid the pitfalls of complacency at home.

And, of course, I use the principles in this book each time I do a shift as a Deputy Sheriff to keep my community, my colleagues, and myself safe.

If this book has done nothing more than raise your awareness of the potential dangers of complacency, you'll already start to notice the benefits to your business and your life.

I have no doubt, though, that you've also begun to identify the areas where you're most at risk to complacency. You've likely also started thinking about how you can apply vigilance to your business and to your life to help fight the complacency that lurks in the shadows of your successes.

The bonus is that you now also have 10 specific vigilance strategies, battle tested in law enforcement, that you can use to not only identify complacency but to also defeat it. I wish you the best of luck!

Until our paths cross again, be safe, be happy, be healthy.

And be vigilant. Always.

Thanks so much for reading *Be Vigilant!*

—*Len*

NEXT STEPS

 While it's fresh, please leave a review at Amazon, Barnes & Noble, GoodReads, or your favorite retailer! This is among the greatest gifts you can give an author!

 Sign up for the ***Be Vigilant! Newsletter***

Get access to even more vigilance tips, stories, interviews, live-streams, and more!

Sign up here: **BeVigilantBook.com/NewsletterSignup/**

Endnotes

1   Tim Ross and Emily Ashton, "The U.K.'s Next Covid Challenge Could Be Complacency," Bloomberg, March 12, 2021, https://www.bloomberg.com/news/articles/2021-03-13/the-u-k-s-next-covid-challenge-could-be-complacency.

2   Amelia Lucas and Kate Rogers, "McDonald's slams ex-CEO as 'morally bankrupt' after he asks for dismissal of chain's lawsuit against him," CNBC, August 31, 2020, https://www.cnbc.com/2020/08/31/mcdonalds-slams-ex-ceo-as-morally-bankrupt-after-he-asks-for-suit-dismissal.html.

3   "Complacency," Merriam-Webster, accessed February 12, 2021, https://www.merriam-webster.com/dictionary/complacency.

4   "Shooter Who Ambushed Philadelphia Police Officer Gets Up to 97 Years," NBC Philadelphia, May 14, 2018, https://www.nbcphiladelphia.com/news/local/edward-archer-sentence-philadelphia-police-officer-jesse-hartnett-sentence/188679/.

5   Douglas County Sheriff's Office, Facebook, January 5, 2015, https://fr-fr.facebook.com/DouglasCountySheriff/photos/ever-dream-about-working-in-law-enforcement-our-reserve-deputy-program-lets-you-/10153522881951040/.

6   "Vital Signs: Alcohol-Impaired Driving Among Adults — United States 2010," *Morbidity and Mortality Weekly Report* (MMWR) 60, no. 39 (2011), https://www.cdc.gov/mmwr/preview/mmwrhtml/mm6039a4.htm.

7   Tom Massmann, "11-year-old girl on sled dies after slamming into the truck towing her," KRDO, November 28, 2020, https://krdo.com/news/top-stories/2020/11/28/11-year-old-girl-on-sled-dies-after-slamming-into-the-truck-towing-her/.

8   FBI, "Killed in the Line of Duty: A Study of Selected Felonious Killings of Law Enforcement Officers," US Department of Justice, 1992, https://www.ojp.gov/library/abstracts/killed-line-duty-study-selected-felonious-killings-law-enforcement-officers.

9   Therea Agovino, "How much is a NYC taxi medallion worth these days?" CBS News, April 17, 2017, https://www.cbsnews.com/news/how-much-is-a-nyc-taxi-medallion-worth-these-days/.

10   Brian O'Connell, "The History of Uber: Timeline and Facts," TheStreet, July 23, 2019, https://www.thestreet.com/technology/history-of-uber-15028611.

11   Jessica McBride, "John Hubert Highnote: 5 Fast Facts You Need to Know," Heavy, December 27, 2018, https://heavy.com/news/2018/04/john-hubert-highnote-bell-gilchrist-suspect/.

12   "6 people face charges after 2 off-duty Montreal police officers assaulted," CBC News, August 27, 2019, https://www.cbc.ca/news/canada/montreal/montreal-police-assault-4-charged-1.5260955.

13   Matt Skoufalos, "Camden County Police: Shooters Targeted Off-Duty Cops, Newborn, in Their Home," NJ Pen, September 17, 2020, https://www.njpen.com/camden-county-police-shooters-targeted-off-duty-cops-newborn-in-their-home/.

14   Bobby Welber, "DA: Police Officers in Hudson Valley are Getting Harassed at Home," Hudson Valley Post, September 23, 2020, https://hudsonvalleypost.com/da-police-officers-in-hudson-valley-are-getting-harassed-at-home/.

15   "About Tesla," Tesla, accessed February 23, 2021, https://www.tesla.com/about.

16   Robert Coran, *Boyd: The Fighter Pilot Who Changed the Art of War* (New York, NY: Back Bay Books, 2002).

17   Harry Hillaker, "Tribute to John R. Boyd," *Code One* magazine, July 1997, https://www.codeonemagazine.com/f16_article.html?item_id=156.

18   Daniel Negreanu, "Advice by Daniel Negreanu: Limping in with pocket aces may get more chips," Tucson.com, November 9, 2006, https://tucson.com/entertainment/advice-by-daniel-negreanu-limping-in-with-pocket-aces-may-get-more-chips/article_ae03b7b4-e68f-5c45-a756-21b3d89fbf54.html.

19   Mike Triplett, "Inside the NFL's gutsiest playcall: Saints' Super Bowl XLIV onside kick," ESPN, February 7, 2020, https://www.espn.com/nfl/story/_/id/28261593/inside-nfl-gutsiest-playcall-saints-super-bowl-xliv-onside-kick.

20   Daphne Howland, "Eddie Bauer, PacSun combined under new operating company," RetailDive, June 8, 2018, https://www.retaildive.com/news/eddie-bauer-pacsun-combined-under-new-operating-company/525282/.

21   Todd Spangler, "'Tiger King' Nabbed Over 34 Million U.S. Viewers in First 100 Days, Nielsen Says," *Variety*, April 8, 2020, https://variety.com/2020/digital/news/tiger-king-nielsen-viewership-data-stranger-things-1234573602/.

22   "Jan 13, 1888 CE: National Geographic Society Founded," National Geographic, accessed February 15, 2021, https://www.nationalgeographic.org/thisday/jan13/national-geographic-society-founded/.

23   Coburn Dukehart, "'National Geographic' Celebrates 125 Years of Photography," NPR, October 1, 2013, https://www.npr.org/sections/

pictureshow/2013/10/01/227871549/national-geographic-celebrates-125-years-of-photography.

24 Jim Motavalli, "About Face: Companies That Reinvented Themselves," *Success* magazine, November 19, 2013, https://www.success.com/about-face-companies-that-reinvented-themselves/.

25 Kayleigh Barger, "'Keep an open mind and take some risks': How National Geographic is adapting its Instagram feed," Digiday, June 1, 2020, https://digiday.com/media/keep-an-open-mind-and-take-some-risks-how-the-national-geographic-is-adapting-its-instagram-feed/.

26 Rebecca Skilbeck, "Talent Mobility: The Key to Unlocking Your Organization's Potential," *Forbes*, May 30, 2019, https://www.forbes.com/sites/rebeccaskilbeck/2019/05/30/talent-mobility-the-key-to-unlocking-your-organizations-potential/?sh=4cb041934ace.

27 Brian Costello, "Peyton Manning's one skill that hasn't decreased with age," *New York Post*, February 2, 2016, https://nypost.com/2016/02/02/peyton-mannings-one-skill-that-hasnt-decreased-with-age/.

28 Zak Keefer, "The best Peyton Manning stories you've never heard," IndyStar, updated October 5, 2017, https://www.indystar.com/story/sports/nfl/colts/2017/10/04/peyton-manning-best-stories-youve-never-heard/731585001/.

29 Waldo Waldman, "Are You Mission Ready?" Wingman, accessed February 15, 2021, https://yourwingman.com/home-video-3/.

30 "Debriefing for Clinical Learning," Agency for Healthcare Research and Quality (AHRQ), updated September 2019, https://psnet.ahrq.gov/primer/debriefing-clinical-learning.

31 Eric Deggans, "Let's Be Careful Out There: The Legacy of 'Hill Street Blues,'" NPR, May 8, 2014, https://www.npr.org/2014/05/08/310742743/lets-be-careful-out-there-the-legacy-of-hill-street-blues/.

32 Clarissa Sievers, "Pepsi or Coke? An In-Depth Look at Decades of Marketing Rivalry," Pinckney, February 23, 2020, https://pinckneymarketing.com/coke-vs-pepsi-rivalry/.

33 "Pepsi Statement Re: Pepsi Moments Content," PepsiCo, April 5, 2017, https://www.pepsico.com/news/press-release/pepsi-statement-re—pepsi-moments-content04052017.

34 Maggie Astor, "Dove Drops an Ad Accused of Racism," the *New York Times*, October 8, 2017, https://www.nytimes.com/2017/10/08/business/dove-ad-racist.html.

35 Rick Reilly, "Paint Like a Champion," ESPN, December 21, 2012, https://www.espn.com/espn/story/_/id/8765862/notre-dame-play-champion-today-sign.

36   Greg Tourney, "PLAY LIKE A CHAMPION TODAY," Notre Dame, November 12, 2004, https://und.com/play-like-a-champion-today/.

37   Chuck Cohn, "A Beginner's Guide to Upselling and Cross-Selling," *Forbes*, May 12, 2015, https://www.forbes.com/sites/chuckcohn/2015/05/15/a-beginners-guide-to-upselling-and-cross-selling/?sh=1c72f11c2912.

38   David Allen, *Getting Things Done: The Art of Stress-Free Productivity* (New York, NY: Penguin, 2002).

39   Dalmeet Singh Chawla, "To Remember, the Brain Must Actively Forget," *Quanta Magazine*, July 24, 2018, https://www.quantamagazine.org/to-remember-the-brain-must-actively-forget-20180724/.

40   Lena Fireston, "Thinking Positively: Why You Need to Wire Your Brain to Think Positive," Psych Alive, accessed February 12, 2021, https://www.psychalive.org/thinking-positively/.

41   Jamie Ducharme, "Here's Why You Can Shut Out the Shock of Mass Shootings," *TIME*, January 24, 2018, https://time.com/5116457/kentucky-marshall-county-shooting-desensitization/.

42   Sara Weisfeldt and Polo Sandoval, "Married cops prove together they could beat deadly odds," CNN, December 29, 2017, https://www.cnn.com/2017/12/29/us/beyond-the-call-of-duty-colorado-dan-brite/index.html.

43   Clayton Sandell, et al., "Colorado officers describe what happened in horrific 'ambush style attack' that killed one of their own," ABC News, May 15, 2018, https://abcnews.go.com/US/colorado-officers-describe-happened-horrific-ambush-style-attack/story?id=5510275.

44   Denis Ucbasaran, Paul Westhead, and Mike Wright, "Why Serial Entrepreneurs Don't Learn from Failure," *Harvard Business Review*, April 2011, https://hbr.org/2011/04/why-serial-entrepreneurs-dont-learn-from-failure.

45   *Memento*, dir. Christopher Nolan (Summit Entertainment, 2000), 113 mins.

46   Todd Rogers and Katherine L. Milkman, "Reminders Through Association," *Psychological Science* 27, 7. 973–986, May 20, 2016, https://doi.org/10.1177/0956797616643071.

47   Pauline Dewan, "Words Versus Pictures: Leveraging the Research on Visual Communication," *The Canadian Journal of Library and Information Practice and Research* 10, no. 1, https://journal.lib.uoguelph.ca/index.php/perj/article/view/3137.

48   Below 100 homepage, accessed February 12, 2021, https://www.below100.org/.

49   Anthony D'Allessandro, "EMMYS: Mike Judge On How Viacom-Paramount Merger Influenced 'Silicon Valley' & 'Office Space's Impact on TGI Fridays," Deadline/Yahoo! Entertainment, June 14, 2014, https://www.yahoo.com/

entertainment/news/emmys-mike-judge-viacom-paramount-merger-influenced-silicon-224521745.html.

50   David Meerman Scott and Brian Halligan, *Marketing Lessons from the Grateful Dead: What Every Business Can Learn From the Most Iconic Band in History* (Hoboken, NJ: Wiley, 2010).

51   Baran Metin, "HR analytics: autonomy and employee engagement," Effectory, August 23, 2019, https://www.effectory.com/knowledge/hr-analytics-autonomy-and-employee-engagement/.

52   "Survey: More Than Half of Employees Have Worked for a Micromanager," Robert Half, July 1, 2014, http://rh-us.mediaroom.com/2014-07-01-Survey-More-Than-Half-of-Employees-Have-Worked-for-a-Micromanager.

53   Ann M Graybiel, "Habits, rituals, and the evaluative brain," *Annual Review of Neuroscience* 31 (2008), https://doi.org/10.1146/annurev.neuro.29.051605.112851.

54   Benjamin Gardner, et al., "Making health habitual: the psychology of 'habit-formation' and general practice," *British Journal of General Practice* 62, no. 605 (December 2012), https://doi.org/10.1146/annurev.neuro.29.051605.112851.

55   "Video: Body cam captures moments leading up to killing of Ariz. cop," Police1, January 13, 2015, https://www.police1.com/officer-shootings/articles/video-body-cam-captures-moments-leading-up-to-killing-of-ariz-cop-8LtP6d3U6lHfn2pH/.

56   Jim Walsh, "911 tapes: Suspect called police before shooting Flagstaff officer," *The Republic*, azcentral.com, https://www.azcentral.com/story/news/local/arizona/2015/01/02/flagstaff-officer-murder-911-tapes-abrk/21194935/.

57   "Big Mistake… Don't Judge a Book by its Cover," Shep Hyken, September 2017, https://hyken.com/customer-service-culture/big-mistake-dont-judge-book-buy-its-cover/.

58   Megan Brenan, "Amid Pandemic, Confidence in Key U.S. Institutions Surges," Gallup, August 12, 2020, https://news.gallup.com/poll/317135/amid-pandemic-confidence-key-institutions-surges.aspx.

59   "Americans' Views of Government: Low Trust, but Some Positive Performance Ratings," Pew Research Center, September 14, 2020, https://www.pewresearch.org/politics/2020/09/14/americans-views-of-government-low-trust-but-some-positive-performance-ratings/.

60   "Trust in government: 1958-2015," Pew Research Center, November 23, 2015, https://www.pewresearch.org/politics/2015/11/23/1-trust-in-government-1958-2015/.

61   "2020 Edelman Trust Barometer," Edelman, January 19, 2020, https://apnews.com/article/shootings-police-chicago-crime-u-s-news-428c2fba22b418280ef3c07acf4bc39c.

62 Don Babwin, "Lack of body cameras fuels suspicion in Chicago shooting," Associated Press, August 11, 2020, https://apnews.com/article/shootings-police-chicago-crime-u-s-news-428c2fba22b418280ef3c07acf4bc39c.

63 Ibid.

64 Ibid.

65 Richard Fausset and Sheila Dewan, "Elijah McClain Died After He Was Detained. Now He's Being Remembered," the *New York Times*, updated June 30, 2020, https://www.nytimes.com/2020/06/20/us/elijah-mcclain-police-killings.html.

66 "Enhance Law Enforcement Integrity," Colorado General Assembly, accessed February 15, 2021, https://leg.colorado.gov/bills/sb20-217.

67 "State Law Enforcement Body Camera Policies," epic.org, accessed February 23, 2021, https://epic.org/state-policy/police-cams/.

68 Kimberly Amadeo, "Causes of the 2008 Global Financial Crisis," The Balance, updated May 29, 2020, https://www.thebalance.com/what-caused-2008-global-financial-crisis-3306176.

69 Nick Lioudis, "The Collapse of Lehman Brothers: A Case Study," Investopedia, updated January 30, 2021, https://www.investopedia.com/articles/economics/09/lehman-brothers-collapse.asp.

70 "H.R.4173 - Dodd-Frank Wall Street Reform and Consumer Protection Act," Congress.gov., accessed February 15, 2021, https://www.congress.gov/bill/111th-congress/house-bill/4173.

71 "2012 Edelman Trust Barometer," Edelman, January 23, 2012, https://www.edelman.com/trust/2012-trust-barometer.

72 "2020 Edelman Trust Barometer."

73 "Facebook Reports First Quarter 2020 Results," Facebook, April 29, 2020, https://investor.fb.com/investor-news/press-release-details/2020/Facebook-Reports-First-Quarter-2020-Results/default.aspx.

74 Sam Shead, "Facebook owns the four most downloaded apps of the decade," BBC News, December 18, 2019, https://www.bbc.com/news/technology-50838013.

75 Claire Rielly, "Mark Zuckerberg defends Facebook's ad model: 'We don't sell people's data," CNET January 24, 2019, https://www.cnet.com/news/mark-zuckerberg-defends-facebook-advertising-model-we-dont-sell-peoples-data/.

76 Tweet by @SethS_D, March 29, 2018, https://twitter.com/SethS_D/status/979430917906321409.

77 Charlie Osborne, "Facebook's worst privacy scandals and data disasters," ZDNet, February 1, 2019, https://www.zdnet.com/pictures/all-of-facebooks-privacy-and-data-snafus-in-recent-history/.

78   Natasha Lomas, "Facebook data misuse and voter manipulation back in the frame
      with latest Cambridge Analytica leaks," Tech Crunch, January 6, 2020, https://
      techcrunch.com/2020/01/06/facebook-data-misuse-and-voter-manipulation-back-
      in-the-frame-with-latest-cambridge-analytica-leaks/.

79   Tiffany Hsu and Eleanor Lutz, "More Than 1,000 Companies Boycotted Facebook.
      Did It Work?" the *New York Times*, August 1, 2020, https://www.nytimes.
      com/2020/08/01/business/media/facebook-boycott.html.

80   "The infinite dial 2020," Edison Research, March 19, 2020, https://www.
      edisonresearch.com/the-infinite-dial-2020/.

81   "Study #19093," NBC News/the *Wall Street Journal*, March 23–7, 2019, https://
      www.documentcloud.org/documents/5794861-19093-NBCWSJ-March-Poll-4-5-
      19-Release.html.

82   Walter Pavlo, "Character Is What you DO When EVERYONE Is Watching," *Forbes*,
      October 23, 2012, https://www.forbes.com/sites/walterpavlo/2012/10/23/character-
      is-what-you-do-when-everyone-is-watching/?sh=168fdaffc6d3.

83   Sharam Ahari, "I was a drug rep. I know how Pharma companies pushed
      opioids," the *Washington Post*, November 26, 2019, https://www.washingtonpost.
      com/outlook/i-was-a-drug-rep-i-know-how-pharma-companies-pushed-
      opioids/2019/11/25/82b1da88-beb9-11e9-9b73-fd3c65ef8f9c_story.html.

84   Courtney Sexton, "The Accidental Invention of the Slip 'N Slide," *Smithsonian*
      magazine, July 2, 2020, https://www.smithsonianmag.com/innovation/accidental-
      invention-slip-n-slide-180975236/.

85   Charles M. Katz, et al., "Evaluating the Impact of Officer Worn Body Cameras
      in the Phoenix Police Department," ASU Center for Violence Prevention and
      Community Safety, December 2014, https://publicservice.asu.edu/sites/default/files/
      ppd_spi_feb_20_2015_final.pdf.

86   Anthony Braga, et al., "Benefits of Body-Worn Cameras: New Findings from a
      Randomized Controlled Trial at the Las Vegas Metropolitan Police Department,"
      US Department of Justice, September 2017, https://www.ojp.gov/library/abstracts/
      benefits-body-worn-cameras-new-findings-randomized-controlled-trial-las-vegas.

87   "Full Metro Council votes to approve civilian review board ordinance for LMPD,"
      WLKY, updated November 19, 2020, https://www.wlky.com/article/full-metro-
      council-votes-to-approve-civilian-review-board-ordinance-for-lmpd/34733287#.

88   Safia Samee Ali, "Voters around the U.S. approve local police reform measures,"
      NBC News, November 4, 2020, https://www.nbcnews.com/politics/2020-election/
      voters-around-u-s-approve-local-police-reform-measures-n1246500.

89   "History," Civilian Complaint Review Board, accessed February 15, 2021, https://
      www1.nyc.gov/site/ccrb/about/history.page.

90 Darrel W. Stephens, et al., "Civilian Oversight of the Police in Major Cities," COPS, 2018, https://cops.usdoj.gov/RIC/Publications/cops-w0861-pub.pdf.

91 Josh Sanburn, "The One Battle Michael Brown's Family Will Win," *TIME*, November 25, 2014, https://time.com/3606376/police-cameras-ferguson-evidence/.

92 Hanna Murphy, "How the viral app Houseparty is entertaining a generation in lockdown," *Financial Times*, March 24, 2020, https://www.ft.com/content/c7ce2ad3-7276-4d8a-9deb-21acca871082/.

93 Tweet by @houseparty, March 30, 2020, https://twitter.com/houseparty/status/1244827034406121472.

94 Kurt Wagner, "Houseparty Vies With Zoom to Be Homebound Chatters' App of Choice," Bloomberg, April 15, 2020, https://www.bloomberg.com/news/articles/2020-04-15/houseparty-vies-with-zoom-to-be-homebound-chatters-app-of-choice.

95 Marcus Sheridan, *They Ask, You Answer: A Revolutionary Approach to Inbound Sales, Content Marketing, and Today's Digital Customer* (Hoboken, NJ: Wiley, 2017).

96 Rebcca Robledo, "Learn More About our PSN Top 50 Builders," Pool Spa News, June 23, 2020, https://www.poolspanews.com/companies/top-50-builders/learn-more-about-our-psn-top-50-builders_o.

97 "America's Women and the Wage Gap," National Partnership for Women and Families, September 2020, https://www.nationalpartnership.org/our-work/resources/economic-justice/fair-pay/americas-women-and-the-wage-gap.pdf.

98 Hailley Griffis, "Pay Analysis Update: Examining Equal Pay at Buffer in 2020," Buffer, April 10, 2020, https://buffer.com/resources/2020-pay-analysis/.

99 Ibid.

100 Samantha Cooney, "Should You Share Your Salary With Co-Workers? Here's What Experts Say," *TIME*, August 14, 2018, https://time.com/5353848/salary-pay-transparency-work/.

101 Chris Weller, "A CEO who makes everyone's salary transparent says people are more productive than ever," Business Insider, May 8, 2017, https://www.businessinsider.com/sumall-ceo-says-salary-transparency-makes-people-more-productive-2017-5.

102 Tony Hsieh, "A Lesson From Zappos: Follow the Golden Rule," *Harvard Business Review*, June 4, 2010, https://hbr.org/2010/06/a-lesson-from-zappos-follow-th.

103 Patagonia website, accessed February 15, 2021, https://www.patagonia.com/home/.

104 "About The Walt Disney Company," The Walt Disney Company, accessed February 15, 2021, https://thewaltdisneycompany.com/about/.

105 Kellogg's website, accessed February 15, 2021, https://www.kelloggcompany.com/en_US/home.html.

106 "Purpose, Vision, and the Southwest Way," Southwest, accessed February 15, 2021, http://investors.southwest.com/our-company/purpose-vision-and-the-southwest-way.

107 Sheila Marikar, "Natasha Richardson Died of Epidural Hematoma After Skiing Accident," ABC News, March 19, 2009, https://abcnews.go.com/Entertainment/Movies/story?id=7119825&page=1.

108 Eric Ries, *The Lean Startup: How Today's Entrepreneurs Use Continuous Innovation to Create Radically Successful Businesses* (New York, NY: Currency, 2011).

109 Malcolm Gladwell, *Blink: The Power of Thinking Without Thinking* (New York, NY: Back Bay Books, 2007).

110 Donald T. Campbell, "Assessing the impact of planned social change," *Evaluation and Program Planning* 2, no. 1, https://doi.org/10.1016/0149-7189(79)90048-X.

111 Marilyn Strathern, "'Improving ratings': audit in the British University System," *European Review* 5, no. 3 (July 1997), https://doi.org/10.1002/(SICI)1234-981X(199707)5:3<305::AID-EURO184>3.0.CO;2-4.

112 Las Vegas, Nevada to Denver, Colorado, Travelmath, accessed February 15, 2021, https://www.travelmath.com/flying-time/from/Denver,+CO/to/Las+Vegas,+NV

113 James W. Popham, "Educator Cheating on No Child Left Behind Tests," *Education Week*, April 18, 2006, https://www.edweek.org/teaching-learning/opinion-educator-cheating-on-no-child-left-behind-tests/2006/04.

114 Ibid.

115 Anne-Laure Le Cunff, "The Cobra Effect: how linear thinking leads to unintended consequences," Ness Labs, accessed February 15, 2021, https://nesslabs.com/cobra-effect.